Lean & Green Cookbook

Breakfast Lunch Dinner Recipes Transform Your Health Built Confidence Quick Weight Maintenance 7-Day Meal Plan for Life-Long Success.

By

Matthew A. Smith

© **Copyright 2021 by Matthew A. Smith - All rights reserved.**

This document is geared towards providing exact and reliable information in regard to the topic and issue covered. The publication is sold with the idea that the publisher is not required to render accounting, officially permitted, or otherwise, qualified services. If advice is necessary, legal or professional, a practiced individual in the profession should be ordered.

From a Declaration of Principles which was accepted and approved equally by a Committee of the American Bar Association and a Committee of Publishers and Associations.

In no way is it legal to reproduce, duplicate, or transmit any part of this document in either electronic means or in printed format. Recording of this publication is strictly prohibited and any storage of this document is not allowed unless with written permission from the publisher. All rights reserved.

The information provided herein is stated to be truthful and consistent, in that any liability, in terms of inattention or otherwise, by any usage or abuse of any policies, processes, or directions contained within is the solitary and utter responsibility of the recipient reader. Under no circumstances will any legal responsibility or blame be held against the publisher for any reparation, damages, or monetary loss due to the information herein, either directly or indirectly.

Respective authors own all copyrights not held by the publisher.

The information herein is offered for informational purposes solely and is universal as so. The presentation of the information is without contract or any type of guarantee assurance.

The trademarks that are used are without any consent, and the publication of the trademark is without permission or backing by the trademark owner. All trademarks and brands within this book are for clarifying purposes only and are owned by the owners themselves, not affiliated with this document.

Table of contents

INTRODUCTION 6

CHAPTER 1: INTRODUCTION TO OPTAVIA DIET 8

1.1 History and Origin of Optavia Diet 8

1.2 Optavia Diet According to Nutrition and Dietetics 10

1.3 The Basic Working Principle and Science behind Optavia Diet 11

1.4 Advantages of Optavia Diet 12

CHAPTER 2: FACTORS TO CONSIDER BEFORE STARTING THE OPTAVIA DIET 17

2.1 Planning your Optavia Diet 18

2.2 Creating a Diet That Works to Reduce Weight 19

2.3 Why should you follow the Optavia Diet? 21

2.4 Role of Exercise along with the Diet 22

CHAPTER 3: WEIGHT MAINTENANCE AND MEAL PLAN 24

3.1 Optavia Diet 7 Days Meal Plan 26

3.2 Self-Monitoring Your Weight 30

3.3 Motivating Yourself 33

3.4 Keeping Yourself Sound and Healthy 37

CHAPTER 4: OPTAVIA DIET- SHOPPING LIST AND RECIPES 40

4.1 Grocery List- Foods You Need to Start the Diet 40

4.2 Optavia Breakfast Recipes 43

4.3 Lunch Recipes 63

4.4 Dinner Recipes 92

4.5 Recipes for Juices, Sweet Dishes and Salads 121

CONCLUSION 158

Introduction

Being on a "Strict Diet" is a term generally heard when we look into the lives of supermodels, entertainers, artists, thus numerous others in the showbiz. Though, currently people use different diet plans to cope with their health. Even people with a normal daily life routine want to lose weight and call themselves healthy and smart.

Ordinary people really start imitating their stars. They always want to live the lives of their ideals and they also want to look like them in the first place. You may have come across many celebrity stars in magazines, different internet blogs mentioning people who have lost enormous weight, and people are going nuts around them asking them how they lost so many pounds. Every person wants to know their diet regime and the secret behind their glowing skin and glamorous body.

This book will introduce you to a new diet therapy that you can efficiently and effectively follow at home. You may not need to head up to a nutritionist or a dietician and pay them to make you a diet plan. You can also get to know the history and science behind an optavia diet and better understand the concept before you start rushing your body towards dieting. Optavia diet includes three different types of diet plans and each of them results in effective weight loss. Optavia diet comprises of meals that make a 1000-1200 calorie meal per day.

This book will help you explore your body's needs and will help you address the facts behind good and healthy eating. Remember, as a healthy individual, you do not have to just focus on your eating habits.

Still, also being active and doing regular exercises can also help you lose pounds and give a healthy start to your life. You will feel fresh and full of life once you start listening to the little signs your body gives you, which we usually neglect.

This book will give you not just the information regarding the Optavia Diet but, it will also provide you with natural homemade recipes that you can make and help you with healthy eating, following these recipes you will find yourself like those foods also that you once deemed unpleasant. Different exercises, as well as diet plans, will be introduced to you that you may start following right away.

Foods that are healthy for your body and give you energy, as well as foods that will help you burn your fat molecules easily, are also listed in this book, you can easily choose your favorite foods and skip those that you may have some allergy towards. Becoming the doctor to your own body will not be as difficult as it seems now once you finish reading this book. So, it is time to burn some calories by saying no to unhealthy foods and getting a head start with nutritious as well as delicious meals.

Chapter 1: Introduction to Optavia Diet

Individuals are being attracted everyday towards different diet plans that are actually meal replacement plans. Diet plans may include lowering the carbohydrate level in your daily meals to enhance weight reduction. One well known diet plan is the very famous Optavia Diet.

Optavia diet includes six meals per day, but keeping in mind the quantity of those meals to be extremely low so that your daily calorie count does not exceed 1000 to 1200 calories per day.

Optavia diet also adds a social and mental support component into the plan by providing full access to a fitness and health expert who may help you by encouraging you with your diet routine and guiding you through the entire process.

Now, the point to remember while starting this particular diet plan is that you need to be consistent with your plan. It may become unsustainable once you start leaving this program. You may start gaining weight again, so be consistent and focused on your diet plan.

1.1 History and Origin of Optavia Diet

William Vitale, a clinical specialist, established a company named HealthRite in 1980. He sold his items straightforwardly to different specialists, who then endorsed them to their patients. The organization is traded on an open market on the New York Stock Exchange. On July 17, 1995, HealthRite changed its name to Vitamin Specialties Corp.

In 2001, the organization changed its name to Medifast, Inc. In 2002, Retired Marine Colonel Bradley T. MacDonald and Chairman of the Board at that point, alongside clinical expert Dr. Wayne Scott Andersen, created Take Shape for Life as a personal Coach to Client system and the company's Habits of Health System.

In October 2010, Medifast was positioned number one on Forbes magazine's rundown of "America's 100 Best Small Companies". The organization was positioned eighteenth as of the 2014 rundown. Medifast was named one of Forbes 100 Most Trustworthy Companies in America in 2016 and 2017.

In July 2017, Medifast changed the name of its auxiliary Take Shape for Life to Optavia and presented another line of items, Optavia Essentials, straightforwardly sold from Coaches to customers. On December 31, 2017, OPTAVIA income brought about the ninth back-to-back quarter of development with an absolute number of 16,700 dynamic procuring Optavia Coaches.

In October 2017, Medifast moved its central command to Baltimore from Owings Mills, Maryland. In February 2018, Medifast reported the organization's augmentation of its extensive sound living projects and items into Hong Kong and Singapore in the principal half of 2019 with its way of life brand, Optavia. The organization is public with a market capitalization of $1.4 billion, as of May 2018.

1.2 Optavia Diet According to Nutrition and Dietetics

Like other meal management plans that abstain an individual from food, the Optavia Diet facilitates clients with its own variety of marked items that replace a few meals for the duration of the day. Optavia diet offers meal management plans for objectives of weight reduction and weight upkeep. The Optavia diet is a "5 and 1" plan. This type of Optavia diet plan is the most well-known and is intended for fast weight reduction. In this meal plan, clients eat five of Optavia's "fuelings" and one low-calorie "lean and green" natively constructed meal every single day.

The optavia diet comprises of different plans, the "3 and 3" and "4 and 2 and 1", all these types have different management styles. These plans are most appropriate to the clients who need to get more fit gradually or keep up their present weight. On all of Optavia's plans, both "fuelings" and "lean and green" homemade meals are kept within strict calorie ranges. The Optavia diet plan is composed of six different building blocks that are optimal for health of an individual:

1. Sleep
2. Hydration
3. Mind
4. Motion
5. Surroundings
6. Weight Management

The theory goes that if you have a plan to follow and prescribed small sized meals to eat, you are less likely to stray into unhealthy eating territory.

And when you only eat the limited number of calories the diet provides, sometimes as low as 1,100 calories per day then your weight reduction is guaranteed.

Additionally, another positive point that comes along following this diet plan is that by prepping your own "lean and green" meals each night, healthy home cooking becomes a regular habit, making the transition from the diet back to "regular" healthy eating easier.

Optavia diet also offers a social support component that gives it a unique characteristic as compared to many other meal management plans. Since emotional support is a major factor in weight loss success, those who enroll in its programs have access to a coach, typically someone who has successfully completed the program. This mentor can answer questions, can provide education, and also serve as a cheerleader to you for your weight loss journey.

1.3 The Basic Working Principle and Science behind Optavia Diet

The Optavia diet is a weight reduction or support plan that endorses eating a blend of bought, handled food called fuelings and self-made lean and green dinners. Different clients may add water to powdered food or open up a bar as a feature of six-or-so scaled down suppers every day. The Optavia diet also offers guidance from coaches to help you learn their trademarked habits of health. The plan additionally recommends doing about 30 minutes of moderate intensity exercise per day.

Half of any of the three sorts of Optavia diet is composed of its "fuelings," which incorporate bars, shakes, sweets, grains, and some appetizing choices, similar to soup and crushed potatoes.

These prepared nourishments frequently list soy protein or whey protein as the primary ingredients. Lean and green suppers round out the remainder of the eating regimen, which you can purchase and can also prepare by yourself at home. Those include:

- 3 servings of non-starchy vegetables like lettuce, greens, celery, or cucumbers.
- Up to 2 servings of sound fats like olive oil, olives, or avocado.
- 5 to 7 ounces of cooked lean protein like fish, chicken, egg whites, turkey, or soy.

The Optavia diet plan is what is viewed as a high-protein diet, with protein making up 10–35% of your everyday calories. Nonetheless, the prepared, powdered kind of protein can prompt some not exactly wonderful results. The protein molecules in the diet are quite high which can cause you to feel heavy and have some other undesirable GI results, improving your health with unsweetened Greek yogurt for protein in a smoothie.

1.4 Advantages of Optavia Diet

The Optavia diet plan has additional benefits, as it is easy to follow and offers ongoing support. By limiting sodium intake, it may also help lower blood pressure in some individuals. Following are some advantages of Optavia diet:

1. **This Diet Plan Offers Ongoing Support.**

The Optavia's health mentors are accessible all through the weight reduction and upkeep programs. One scientific examination found a critical connection between the quantity of training meetings on the Optavia 5 and 1 Plan and improved weight reduction.

Moreover, research recommends that having a life mentor or guide may help them in long term weight support.

2. This Diet Plan May Help Individuals with Blood Pressure.

The Optavia meal plans may help improve circulatory strain through weight reduction and restricted sodium intake. While the Optavia diet has not been researched specifically, a 40-week study in 90 people with excess weight or obesity on a similar Medifast program revealed a significant reduction in blood pressure. Additionally, all Optavia meal plans are designed to provide less than 2,300 mg of sodium per day. Although, it is up to you to choose your low sodium options for lean and green meals. Numerous health associations, including the Institute of Medicine, American Heart Association, and United States Department of Agriculture (USDA), recommend consuming less than 2,300 mg of sodium per day. That is because higher sodium intake is linked to an increased risk of high blood pressure and heart disease in salt-sensitive individuals.

3. This Diet Plan is Easy to be followed.

As the diet relies mostly on prepackaged fueling, you are only responsible for cooking one meal per day on the 5 and 1 Plan. Each plan comes with meal logs and sample meal plans to make it easier to follow. While you are encouraged to cook 1 to 3 Lean and Green meals per day, depending on the plan, they are simple to make as the program includes specific recipes and a list of food options. Furthermore, those who are not interested in cooking can buy packaged meals to replace lean and green meals.

4. **This Diet Plan provides additional ways for maintenance.**

The Optavia diet plan provides additional tools to aid weight loss and maintenance, including tips and inspiration via text message, community forums, weekly support calls, and an app that allows you to set meal reminders and track food intake and activity. The company also provides specialized programs for nursing mothers, older adults, teens, and people with diabetes or gout. Although the Optavia diet offers these specialized plans, it is pretty clear that this diet is safe for people with certain medical conditions. Additionally, it should be kept in mind that teenagers and breastfeeding mothers have unique nutrient and calorie needs that may not be met by the Optavia diet plan.

- Improving your Health

We have all had those well-intentioned moments when we resolve to make sweeping lifestyle changes: quit smoking, lose 20 pounds, and join a gym and start exercising every day. While we should always strive to accomplish these types of health goals, the road to better health does not always have to mean making huge leaps. There are also many smaller steps you can take that will help improve your overall health and quality of life and because they are things you can easily incorporate into your routine alongside the Optavia diet plan, they will be easy to maintain for a pretty long period of time. Even if you have only a few minutes to spare, you can use that time to improve your well-being.

Try incorporating the following activities and strategies into your day. When these simple steps become habits, they can add up to a big positive effect on your overall health.

1. A saltshaker on the dining table makes it all too easy to consume excess salt, which can lead to high blood

pressure. So put the shaker in a cabinet or pantry and bring it out only when you are cooking. You can also try spicing up your food with lemon or lime juice, garlic, red pepper flakes, herbs or a salt-free seasoning blend. Stock your fridge and pantry with your favorite fresh and dried herbs so that you will always have them on hand to flavor your foods.

2. Most of us do not get the seven or more hours of sleep that adults need. Over time, a shortage of shut-eye can raise your risk of a heart attack or stroke regardless of your age, weight or exercise habits.

3. Specialists suggest ordinary exercise, and meditation to lessen pressure. Yet, in any event, something as straightforward and agreeable as tuning in to mitigating music, perusing a decent book, soaking yourself in a hot bubble bath or playing with your pet can enable you to unwind from your stresses and relax.

4. Maintaining a healthy weight can lower your risk for heart disease, stroke and some types of cancer. But for women, there is another reason to keep pounds from piling on which is that it will decrease the risk for future pelvic floor disorders. Pelvic floor disorders are more common in women who have delivered babies vaginally. However, a recent study has found that even women who have never had a vaginal birth are at increased risk for urinary stress incontinence if they are overweight or obese.

5. Take a few minutes to stretch out before and after you exercise. If you are not working out that day, take a few

stretch breaks. Find a quiet space in the office where you will not be disturbed. Look for natural opportunities in your daily routine to stretch, such as getting out of your car or reaching for items on a high shelf at the store.

6. Researchers have found that mentally challenging activities, such as reading, doing crossword puzzles or Sudoku and playing chess, may have a protective effect on your brain. According to research studies, regularly engaging your mind may help lower your risk for the dementia associated with Alzheimer's disease. There are other ways to maintain your brain health. Eat with your non-dominant hand. Walk a new route home from work. And connect with others as staying socially engaged may also protect against dementia.

7. Making healthy dietary substitutions such as following the Optavia diet is one of the major steps you need to take to change your life style. Optavia diet can change the course of your life once and for all.

When you are young, you can build the foundation for a lifetime of good health. When you are older, healthy habits can help you control any diseases you have and lower your risk of getting others in the future.

Chapter 2: Factors to Consider Before Starting the Optavia Diet

It appears as though there is consistently a new eating routine in the news every now and then. Furthermore, regardless of how much examination you do on a popular eating regimen, the vast majority actually neglects to remember a couple of critical components and that is one reason why their weight control systems fizzle. Individuals constantly neglect the negative impact that consuming excessively less calories can have on their psychological state. What may begin as a blameless endeavor to get fit can get disengaging or fanatical, which is the reason taking part in abstaining from excessive food intake practices likewise increment the danger of many eating disorders, for example, gorging or purging.

Rolling out comparable improvements will go farther than simply slicing calories or holding fast to another trend diet. Changing a few practices to improve your general wellbeing is an incredible methodology. You can implement a couple of various strategies including, adding more foods grown from the ground to your eating plans as opposed to eliminating something, taking every day walks or organizing your personal time, is very crucial before you start a diet plan.

If your goal is to change your eating habits for the long-term and lose weight, strict dieting might not be your best option. The most important thing to consider before starting a new diet is that diets do not work. Unless the dietary changes you are making are lifestyle changes, you may experience short-term weight loss but the weight regain is likely to occur, and weight regain to an even higher weight than you started with is likely if you are not physically active.

Individuals will in general feel that another eating routine or weight reduction will make their weight troubles go away. However, actually, weighing less does not shield you from difficulties or inconvenience throughout everyday life.

2.1 Planning your Optavia Diet

Point to note that this specific diet is getting the attention of the numerous individuals out of nowhere. By focusing on this eating regimen, you can easily shed roughly many pounds in a couple of days. There are two periods of the Optavia diet, which are as per the following:

Initial Stage:

In the initial stage of the Optavia diet plan, you will firstly choose which type of optavia diet you are going to follow; either it is the 5 and 1, the 4, 2 and 1 or the 3 and 3 diet plans. Once, you choose your diet plan you will start following it on a regular basis without adding any cheat day into the routine. You will observe a change in your life with regards to your life attitudes; you will feel a sense of positivity around you with respect to health and fitness. In this stage you will be introduced to a variety of Optavia meals that you will have to take according to the type of Optavia diet plan you decide to follow. At this stage you are advised to have an intake of only 1000 to 1200 calories and not more.

Transition Stage:

Whenever you have accomplished your solid weight, and have realized what smart dieting really is, you may assist yourself with progressing to long lasting smart dieting that will help you maintain your weight.

The transition stage continuously builds your calorie consumption and once again introduces a more extensive assortment of nourishments. The calories you need after progress to keep up your weight changes as per your weight, height, sex, age, and action level will be detailed in the transition stage. In this stage, the calorie count is different for each individual.

2.2 Creating a Diet That Works to Reduce Weight

There are numerous approaches to lose a ton of weight quickly. These are significant reasons why you may think that it is difficult to kick the bucket. Though not all eating regimens have the same impact. Low carb counts are very important for weight reduction and might be simpler to adhere to than other diets. Following are some points to be noted while preparing a diet for yourself:

1. It should increase the metabolic wellbeing of your body.
2. The diet should essentially diminish your cravings.
3. It should cause fast reduction in weight simultaneously.

You do not have to exercise to get in shape; however, it will have additional advantages. By lifting loads, you will consume heaps of calories and keep your digestion from easing back down, which is a typical symptom of losing weight. Studies on low carbohydrate diets show that by eating fewer carbs you can increase a touch of muscle while losing noteworthy measures of body fat. Try heading off to the gym three to four times each week to lift weights. Both cardio and weightlifting can help with weight reduction.

Eating a lot of protein is a basic building block of a weight loss diet plan. Evidence proposes that eating loads of protein may support calorie consumption by 80-100 calories each day. High protein diets can likewise decrease hunger levels and cause you to feel full. In one examination, individuals on a higher protein diet consumed 441 less calories for every day. With regards to shedding pounds, protein is an important supplement to consider.

Every last one of your meals ought to incorporate a protein source, fat source, and low carbohydrate vegetable source. As a general standard, have a go at eating a few meals every day. If you get yourself hungry toward the evening, include a fourth meal also. Constructing your meals along these lines ought to bring your carb intake down to around 20-50 grams for each day.

As per a few dietitians, it is normal to lose as much as 10 pounds (around 4.5 kg) and sometimes even more in the primary seven day stretch of eating along these lines. This weight reduction incorporates both muscles versus fat and water weight. The research area proposes that a low carbohydrate diet can lower hunger levels, which may lead you towards weakness. Set forth plainly, lowering carbs can prompt speedy and simple weight reduction.

The most significant part is to cut off sugars and starches in your diet. At the point when you do that, your levels of hunger go down automatically, and you, for the most part, wind up eating fewer calories altogether. Rather than consuming carbs for keeping up your energy level, your body currently begins consuming the fat that was previously stored for energy. Another advantage of cutting carbs is that it brings down the insulin levels, making the kidneys shed the excess sodium and water. Try not to fear eating fats. Attempting to do low carb and low-fat diets simultaneously can make adhering to the eating regimen extremely troublesome.

2.3 Why should you follow the Optavia Diet?

The Optavia diet plan is one of those plans that have been skimming around via online media, with a blend of change photographs bragging its adequacy and bounty analysis. Possibly you have come across it while searching for fat reduction strategies and you are interested about whether it would be the correct methodology for you or not.

The Optavia demonstrated Optimal Weight 5 and 1 diet plan kicks off your weight reduction easily and effectively. The deductively demonstrated plans and the items are created by doctors, dietitians, and researchers, and have been utilized by more than a million individuals all around the globe and also by a huge number of medical care suppliers. It is quick, problem free, easy to follow and dependent on the sound propensity for eating six little suppers for each day, one each a few hours. Five of your everyday dinners are Optavia meals. You can choose from the variety of sixty delectable, advantageous, healthfully tradable, logically planned meals.

In this diet plan, your body enters a delicate, however proficient fat-consuming state, which is basic for getting thinner. Each meal contains great protein which holds slender bulk, and furthermore contains probiotic contents, which help uphold stomach related wellbeing, as a component of a decent eating regimen and solid way of life. Additionally, with your five meals, you get familiar with another sound propensity i.e., the technique to make a lean and green supper for yourself and your family.

The Optavia Optimal Weight 4 and 2 and 1 diet plan is ideal for you in the event that you incline towards an adaptable supper intend to assist you with reaching your desirable weight. It can address the issues of a wide scope of people.

It is reasonable for you if you have type 2 diabetes, have under 15 pounds to lose, have type 1 diabetes and you have been firmly checked by the medical services supplier, you exercise more than 45 minutes out of every day, you need to consolidate all of the nutrition classes, including organic product, dairy, and starches into your diet, or are 65 years or more and not routinely physically active.

The Optavia Optimal Health 3 and 3 diet plan assists you with continuing your healthy weight. This diet plan centers around health, little suppers each eaten after a gap of a few hours, while incorporating more food decisions in the correct segments. It is anything but difficult to follow the optimal health 3 and 3 Plan, simply devour three optimal health snacks and three adjusted suppers every day.

So, as you read above the three different types of Optavia diet which can be used according to your medical and health condition. The Optavia diet helps to change your life drastically and gives you a healthy and positive life.

2.4 Role of Exercise along with the Diet

Remaining healthy is at the highest point of everybody's need list, and our day-by-day decisions can decide exactly how healthy we are. Not all things are in our control; however, the propensities and approaches we take to our well-being can frequently have any kind of effect between being healthy and unhealthy. Two regions have the most power over our health, and those are our eating regimen and exercise. These both can easily affect our well-being and can play a role as being the primary factors in forestalling sickness and different problems further down the road. Preventive social and health techniques like appropriate eating routine and exercise can likewise support your spending plan.

The most significant advantage of an incredible eating regimen and normal exercise is the manner in which it enables your body to fight off infections and different conditions. Your body's insusceptible framework is an unpredictable machine, and diet and exercise can vigorously influence it. An excessive number of intakes of inappropriate foods can put you in danger; however, the correct food sources, when supplemented with workout can really support your body's capacity to battle sickness. Both your eating regimen and exercise, particularly the later, affect your state of mind. Synthetic chemicals in the cerebrum called endorphins may help you feel upbeat and positive, and these are activated by many types of exercise activity.

Diet can have a considerable number of similar impacts, and there are many professionals out there proposing that appropriate eating regimen and exercise are two main considerations in generally maintaining psychological wellness. Both of them lessen pressure and can build cerebrum action. Endorphin incitement can likewise help forestall melancholy and raise confidence.

Sleep issues are a worry for many individuals around the world, and diet and exercise can impact your rest propensities. Exercise, specifically, can legitimately affect your capacity to nod off and stay unconscious. It is suggested that you do not practice vigorously or eat directly before sleep time; yet appropriate propensities in the two zones can transform anxious evenings into delightful ones. If you are attempting to improve your activity and dietary propensities, have a sound sleep every night.

You ought to focus on over two hours of medium-force exercise every week, or a somewhat low quantity of high-power work out. Blending vigorous exercise in with things like weight preparation or sports is an incredible method to change your exercises. Make a point to stretch out your body when working out and avoid potential risks.

Chapter 3: Weight Maintenance and Meal Plan

Grievously, various people who get fit breeze up improving their weight once more. The truth is that, pretty much 20% of individuals who start off overweight end up successfully getting fit as a fiddle and keeping it off eventually. Regardless of the fact, do not let this demotivate you in any way. There are different deductively exhibited ways that you can use to keep the weight off, from rehearsing activity to taking care of the weight. Here are a few customary reasons why people reestablish the weight they lose. They are, for the most part, identified with unreasonable desires and sentiments of hardship. Following are some of the reasons of the weight gain:

Wrong Attitude: When you consider about an eating standard as a helpful solution, as opposed to a drawn-out response for improving your prosperity, you will undoubtedly give up and recuperate the weight you lost.

Restrictive Eating Regimens: Extreme calorie impediment may slow your absorption; move your yearning controlling hormones, which are the two factors that add to the weight recovery.

Nonappearance of Maintainable Propensities: Many weight control plans rely upon the goal instead of inclinations you can unite into your everyday life. They focus on standards rather than a method of changes in way of life, which may incapacitate you and thwart weight support.

While shedding pounds is difficult for certain people, it is considerably more testing to keep the weight off the body. Many individuals who lose a ton of weight have recovered it two to three years after the fact.

One speculation about recuperating shed pounds is that people who decrease the proportion of calories they usually get fit as a fiddle. This makes it dynamically difficult to get more fit throughout a period of several months.

This makes it progressively hard to get more fit over a time of months. A lower pace of consuming calories may likewise make it simpler to recover weight after a progressively typical eating regimen is continued. Hence, amazingly low-calorie diets and quick weight reductions are not recommended. Losing close to two pounds for every week is suggested. Consolidating long term changes in life are expected to expand the opportunity of fruitful long term weight reduction.

Weight decrease to a sound load for a normal individual can propel clinical preferences. These consolidate lower cholesterol and glucose levels, lower heartbeat, less weight on bones and joints, and less work for the heart. It is critical to maintain weight decrease to get clinical preferences over a long period.

Keeping extra burden off your body requires responsibility and exertion, comparatively as getting more fit does. Weight decrease goals are reached by a mix of changes in eating regimen, dietary principles, and exercise. Unfortunately, in some unprecedented conditions, people go to a bariatric operation.

3.1 Optavia Diet 7 Days Meal Plan

Optavia diet is a very healthy and mazing weight reducing plan. You can follow the diet plan for seven days mentioned below and make your own diet plan using the above recipes for different nourishments and fuelings.

The diet plan mentioned below is the 5 and 1 type of diet plan that you can easily follow at home with all the meals made by yourself at home. The main point to remember is that your calorie count should not exceed 1000 to 1200 calories per day.

Day 1

Breakfast: Wild Blue berry Almond Hot Cereal 110 kcalories

Snack: Vegetable Juice 110 kcalories

Lunch: Chicken Chili 210 kcalories

Snack: Green tea smoothie 183 kcalories

Dinner: Grilled Stuffed Chicken Italiano 164 kcalories

Snack: Raisin Oat Cinnamon Crisp Bar 35 kcalories

Total Calories 812 kcalories

Day 2

Breakfast: Cauliflower Waffles

190 kcalories

Snack: Yoghurt Berry Blast Smoothie 170 kcalories

Lunch: Crab Cakes 120 kcalories

Snack: Green tea smoothie 183 kcalories

Dinner: Swedish Meatballs with Zucchini Noodles 260 kcalories

Snack: Raisin Oat Cinnamon Crisp Bar 35 kcalories

Total Calories 775 kcalories

Day 3

Breakfast: Ham and Vegetable Omelet 162 kcalories

Snack: Vegetable Juice 110 kcalories

Lunch: Kung Pao Chicken 380 kcalories

Snack: Tuna Salad 117 kcalories

Dinner: Grilled Stuffed Chicken Italiano 164 kcalories

Snack: Raisin Oat Cinnamon Crisp Bar 35 kcalories

Total Calories

968 kcalories

Day 4

Breakfast: Wild Blue berry Almond Hot Cereal 110 kcalories

Snack: Mini Peanut Butter Cups 110 kcalories

Lunch: Chicken Chili 210 kcalories

Snack: Green tea smoothie 183 kcalories

Dinner: Bruschetta Grilled Chicken 174 kcalories

Snack: Chocolate Fudge Crisp Bar 162 kcalories

Total Calories 766 kcalories

Day 5

Breakfast: Feta and Spinach Egg Whites 200 kcalories

Snack: Vegetable Juice 110 kcalories

Lunch: Chicken Chili 210 kcalories

Snack: Green tea smoothie 183 kcalories

Dinner: Cheesy Chicken Cauliflower Skillet 210 kcalories

Snack: Raisin Oat Cinnamon Crisp Bar 35 kcalories

Total Calories
      948 kcalories

Day 6

Breakfast: Egg Omelet with Avocado Slices 170 kcalories

Snack: Chia Bliss Smoothie 110 kcalories

Lunch: Herb Crusted Tofu 210 kcalories

Snack: Green tea smoothie
      183 kcalories

Dinner: Grilled Stuffed Chicken Italiano 164 kcalories

Snack: Chocolate Mint Crisp Bar 227 kcalories

Total Calories
      1064 kcalories

Day 7

Breakfast: Muffin less Egg Cup 163 kcalories

Snack: Green tea smoothie

> 183 kcalories
>
> Lunch: Rolled Garlic Creamy Smashed Potato 139 kcalories
>
> Snack: Raisin Oat Cinnamon Crisp Bar 35 kcalories
>
> Dinner: Baked Cod with tomato and Feta 147 kcalories
>
> Snack: Vegetable Juice 110 kcalories
>
> Total Calories 777 kcalories

The diet plan above can be altered by you according to your choices and taste preferences keeping in mind the calorie count of each recipe that you are adding into your diet plan.

3.2 Self-Monitoring Your Weight

Recording your step-by-step weight on a journal as a graph or timetable can help you screen your thriving or will help you with reducing your weight more quickly. Note that observing yourself more regularly as conceivable step by step is not recommended, as ordinary changes are not markers of veritable weight. Conventional checking of your weight is in like manner basic to help you with keeping up your weight in the wake of getting fit as quickly as possible.

Another self-checking procedure, also as food logs and diaries, is keeping a movement log or physical diary. The number of minutes being active, and the sort and level of exertion of actual activity done are to be recorded.

Checking your weight yourself is a huge and essential self-checking behavior to fill in as a badge of one's eating and actual activity penchants.

Despite the fact that it might be hard and here and there demoralizing to weigh yourself while getting thinner, it is prescribed to weigh yourself week after week, ideally outside of your home on a similar scale. Utilizing the scale at the neighborhood gym or exercise office or your primary care physician's office might be more exact than home scales. Though, if this seems ridiculous going somewhere else to check your weight then, it is alright to utilize a home scale.

Commonly, a simple physical movement that does not expand pulse a lot, or change breathing would ordinarily be the pace that you stroll around work or go out to shop. A moderate degree of physical effort is the point at which you are getting somewhat of an expanded heartbeat and breathing rate. Overwhelming or hard degree of physical effort would perspire, expanded pulse just as expanded relaxing. Keep in mind; the physical movement should be possible at once or irregularly for the duration of the day. A significant and regularly overlooked part of activity logs is the degree of perceived effort. Strolling for thirty minutes, at a simple rate contrasted with a hard pace, will bring about various degrees of calories consumed and cardiovascular effect.

Logging action can be a positive analysis or a recommendation to combine more exercise or actual development into your consistently plan. Starting activities may be walking, riding a fixed bike, or swimming at a moderate movement.

Different kinds of activities that can be fun are moving, practice recordings or seat works out. You should attempt to focus on thirty minutes of activity on most days of the week. Numerous individuals attempt to begin with practice on three or four days of the week.

Notwithstanding, if you can make yourself practice the most to the entire days of the week, regardless of whether just for ten to fifteen minutes, it will turn out to be even more an everyday practice for you.

One of the most broadly perceived and huge kinds of self-checking techniques in weight leader programs is keeping a food log, in which individuals record their nourishments, exercises, or beverages when they are consumed. One significant method with food logs is people recording what they eat or drink as it is devoured; else, it may not give an accurate record of the day's admission.

A decent general guideline for food logs is: in the event that you eat it, you compose it. The base data for weight reduction that ought to be kept in food logs is the type, sum, and caloric substance of food or refreshment taken. This gives the capacity to track and help in equalization of the quantity of calories devoured for the duration of the day with the measure of calories exhausted for the duration of the day. Other wholesome data that can be logged incorporates a time of day while eating, fat substance, and starch grams. Disease explicit food logs can likewise be kept. For instance, concentrating on sugar content rather than calories for patients with diabetes mellitus or insulin obstruction.

Another steady instrument in self-checking is keeping a food diary. Food diaries contrast from food logs since they join ordered information progressively. They are valuable if you are attempting to discover conduct reasons or mental perspectives for eating. Depending upon the individual and conduct complexities included, some food journals could incorporate the anxiety, mind-set, or sentiments encompassing eating, movement, area, other ecological or passionate triggers for eating. The more mind boggling or itemized, the better the feedback.

In any case, in the present society, it is practically incomprehensible for a great many people to keep deeply point by point every day food records for a long-time span. Thus, consistency is regularly low with nitty-gritty food journals. By recommending that patients keep a point-by-point food record for a couple of days every week, maybe significant territories of the center for healthful and social or behavioral intervention can be perceived.

Despite the fact that specific diseases and medications shift, social change is the critical key in weight decrease or balance and reduces the peril of afflictions. Self-noticing is a key to lead changes, and there are an enormous number of ways to deal with self-screen. Most importantly, regardless of how you do it, without anyone's help, checking ought to be a significant piece of your weight reduction, weight support, or sound way of life change. At that point, the following stage is to be certain that self-checking converts into positive conduct changes with respect to diet and exercise.

3.3 Motivating Yourself

Starting and sticking to a strong weight decrease plan can every so often seem, by all accounts, to be incredible. Often, people fundamentally do not have the motivation to start or lose their motivation to progress forward. Luckily, motivation is something you can work to increase. Following are a couple of tips and deceives that you can use to keep yourself pushed:

- Self-observing is urgent to weight reduction inspiration and achievement. The examination has discovered that individuals who track their food admission are bound to get more fit and keep up their weight reduction. In any case, to keep a food diary effectively, you should record all that you eat. You can likewise record your feelings in your food diary. This can assist you with distinguishing certain triggers for gorging and assist you with finding more advantageous approaches to adapt. You can keep food diaries on pen and paper or utilize a site or application. They have all been demonstrated compelling.

- Numerous people endeavoring to get more fit just set outcome targets or destinations that should be accomplished towards the end. Usually, an outcome target will be your last target weight. Regardless, focusing on one outcome destination can wreck your motivation. They can regularly feel unnecessarily distant and leave you feeling substantial. A case of a procedure objective is practicing four times each week. An examination in 126 overweight ladies taking an interest in a get-healthy plan found the individuals who were process centered were bound to get thinner and less inclined to go amiss from their eating regimens, contrasted with the individuals who concentrated on weight reduction results alone.

- Various eating regimens and diet plans ensure smart and basic weight decrease. In any case, most professionals propose simply shedding one to two pounds each week. Characterizing far off goals can incite assessments of disappointment and cause you to give up. Out of the blue, characterizing and accomplishing practical destinations prompts slants of accomplishment. Similarly, people who show up at their self-chosen weight decrease targets are bound to keep up their weight decrease for a long period.

- Obviously, portray all the reasons you require to get slenderer and record them. This will help you with keeping yourself submitted and convinced to show up at your weight decrease destinations. Attempt to pursue them every day and use them as an update when enticed to wander from your weight reduction plans. Your reasons could incorporate forestalling diabetes, keeping yourself active with your grandkids, putting your best self forward for an occasion, improving your self-assurance, or fitting into a specific pair of pants. Numerous individuals begin shedding pounds on the grounds that their primary care physician recommended it. Yet, research shows that this is increasingly effective if their weight reduction inspiration originates from the inside.

- Individuals need customary help and positive criticism to remain focused. Inform your nearby loved ones concerning your weight reduction objectives, so they can help boost you and appreciate your achievement. Numerous individuals likewise think that it is accommodating to discover a weight reduction partner. You can turn out to be together, consider each other responsible, and empower each other all through the procedure. Moreover, it tends to be useful to include your accomplice, yet make a point to get support from others as well, for example, your companions. Besides this, consider joining a care group. Both face to face and online care groups have been demonstrated to be very advantageous.

- Ordinary stressors will, in every case, spring up. Discovering approaches to get ready for them and creating appropriate adapting abilities will assist you with remaining spurred regardless of what life tosses your direction. There will consistently be occasions, birthday events, or gatherings to join in.

- Having a good ideal can assist you with remaining motivated to get thinner. Nonetheless, you have to pick the correct sort of a good example to keep yourself focused. Draping an image of a supermodel on your refrigerator will not inspire you after some time. Rather, discover a good example that you can without much of a stretch identify with. Having a relatable and positive good example may help keep you propelled. Maybe you know a companion who has lost a great deal of weight, and they can be your motivation. You can likewise search for motivational online journals or anecdotes about individuals who have effectively shed pounds.

Being convinced to shed pounds is huge for protracted weight decrease accomplishments. People find different components that can keep them roused, so it is fundamental to find what rouses you unequivocally. Make a point to give yourself flexibility and compliment the little triumphs alongside your weight decrease adventure. Besides, do not be reluctant to demand help when required. With the right instruments and support, you can find and stay centered to show up at your weight decrease goals.

3.4 Keeping Yourself Sound and Healthy

Sometimes we give off an impression of being in a pandemic of mental health issues. There are more significant levels of sadness, uneasiness, and other dysfunctional behaviors than at any time in the recent days, especially among youngsters. The central issue is whether there is anything we can do to stay away from these conditions. We, as a whole, know the significance of eating five meals per day or five segments of natural product or vegetable consistently, to keep up our physical wellbeing.

While the science behind the exact number is most likely to some degree questionable, the significance of eating admirably to keep up wellbeing is not in question. Nobody is recommending that it is feasible for everybody to maintain a strategic distance from all emotional wellness issues. In any case, numerous researchers would state concur that there are things that should be possible to keep up a solid brain.

There is a whole other world to emotional wellness and a great mind than essentially staying away from dementia and other psychological sicknesses. The psyche is formed by all the encounters, thoughts, and considerations to which it is uncovered. To a limited degree, at that point, you can pick what you feed your psyche; similarly, as you can pick what you feed your body. What you decide to devour for your brain can be depicted as your mind diet.

There is developing proof that there is a solid relationship between cell phone use, especially web-based social networking use, and poor psychological well-being. It is not totally clear what causes the connection.

Notwithstanding, there is an extensive hypothesis that web-based social networking drives individuals to make correlations between their own life, and the cautiously curated lives that they see on screen. It is hard not to feel that what is introduced via web-based networking media is reality.

There has been a lot of hypothesis in the press over numerous years about valuable approaches to hinder mind degeneration in old age and, especially, how it may be conceivable to defeat Alzheimer's infection and dementia. One recommendation is that doing crosswords, and different riddles or mind preparing games that keep your cerebrum dynamic may be useful. However, this is probably going to be far less accommodating than physical exercise. This is on the grounds that doing puzzles utilizes just a little piece of your cerebrum and does not do anything for the rest.

We do not generally comprehend what is behind the useful impacts of the activity. In any case, researchers have seen that exercise activity causes all the veins in the body, even for your mind, to expand. This enhances the metabolic limit of the mind. Exercise additionally causes the brain to discharge certain synthetic chemicals that help keep neurons sound and ready to change. This seems like an excellent thing for the cerebrum and the body.

A decent eating routine is basic for physical wellbeing. A developing group of proof recommends that it additionally has any kind of effect on your brain. The Mental Health Foundation takes note of the fact that a decent eating regimen is significant for psychological wellness.

It additionally recommends that diet can assume a job in the turn of events, the board, and avoidance of a few explicit conditions, including schizophrenia, sorrows, consideration deficiency hyperactivity issues (ADHD), and Alzheimer's infection.

This should not imply that diet can control these conditions, nor that it ought to be viewed as a panacea or fix all, or that different medicines ought to be halted for a specific eating routine. However, the diet may assume a job, close by various medications, in the administration of these conditions.

Obviously, similarly, as a physical disease can influence anybody, so can psychological instability, paying little heed to a way of life. Although, if it influences you, you ought to consistently counsel a specialist. No one is recommending that you can fix psychological instability by essentially expending the correct eating routine and taking activity despite the fact that this can add to the administration of your condition.

Science does, anyway, recommend that there are numerous things that we can never really make up our mind and body as solid as could reasonably be expected and add to improved results in case of a disease. Sound judgment recommends that it is generally simple to eat a decent eating routine and take work out and that the advantages to both mental and physical wellbeing. Killing your cell phone occasionally is likewise liable to deliver profits in this term.

Chapter 4: Optavia Diet- Shopping List and Recipes

Studies have demonstrated that food products high in proteins that manage metabolic and different cell capacities may assume a job in expanding our life span, diminishing irritation, and possibly helping in weight reduction too. In case you are apprehensive that this eating regimen plan will be miserably prohibitive, luck is by your side. These metabolic function enhancing foods are not just loaded with amazing polyphenols; they are likewise diverse, scrumptious, and can be added to your meals in various innovative manners.

4.1 Grocery List- Foods You Need to Start the Diet

Following is the list of foods that you can eat as they are very healthy. Many benefits of Optavia diet other than the weight loss properties benefits have already been mentioned in the previous chapters:

Red Wine:

Known as one of the superfoods, red wine has cell fortifications, and even threatening development doing combating potential. Created utilizing purple grape skins and seeds, this reward is high in polyphenols and resveratrol, which can help shield veins from hurt, reduce horrendous cholesterol, and hinder blood bunches. Stick to one glass a day to get the benefits.

Chilies:

It has a critical role in extending the processing of the body. Subsequently, your inside temperature level would rise. In order to bring back the body to the ideal temperature, your body will devour more calories, subsequently quickening the assimilation rate.

Fast assimilation, fitting retention, and waste evacuation can lessen the chance of fat storing up in the body.

Walnuts:

Walnuts can be added to servings of blended greens, pastas, breakfast oats, soups, and arranged products. These nuts are affluent in omega-3 fats and contain higher proportions of disease avoidance than numerous other food items. Eating them may improve cerebrum prosperity and delay coronary ailment and infection.

Arugula leaves:

While an overall invigorating, vegetable-rich eating routine diminishes a person's harmful development danger. Studies have shown that arugula leaves can have unequivocal anticancer and weight decrease properties.

Onions:

Red onions are not simply a low-calorie, flavor-boosting development to any dinner. They may moreover lessen your threat of developing explicit illnesses, due to the compound quercetin. Onions are a basic wellspring of malignancy anticipation specialists and are copious in nutrient C, which gives your immune structure a welcomed uphold.

Coffee:

Close by giving you a shock of energy, it can moreover extend your strength when working out, lessen your peril of explicit diseases, and conceivably improve cerebrum work.

Blueberries:

Blueberries have been found to help lower the dreadful cholesterol level, decline exacerbation in the body, and help you with burning the fat atoms. This yummy berry is a snack you can like each and every day.

Celery:

This may likewise give many benefits to the stomach. Gelatin based polysaccharides in celery, including a compound known as apiuman, have been seemed to lessen events of stomach ulcers, and improve the covering of the stomach.

Kale:

Kale contains fiber, cell fortifications, calcium, C and K nutrients, iron, and a wide extent of various enhancements that can help prevent distinctive clinical issues. A cell fortification assists the body with unfortunate harms that are the result of normal methodology and biological loads.

Soy:

Eating soy is an unfathomable technique to assemble your plant protein. Assessments show that having more plant protein for your eating routine, instead of more sugar, has clear cardiovascular favorable circumstances, for instance, reducing your heartbeat rate. Nourishments containing soy are ordinarily without cholesterol and low in inundated fat. Food with animal proteins high in submerged fat and cholesterol increases your risk of making cardiovascular ailment.

Strawberries:

These solid little packages secure your heart, increase High Density Lipoprotein cholesterol, cut down your heartbeat, and guard against threatening development. Squeezed with supplements, fiber, and particularly raised degrees of cell fortifications known as polyphenols, strawberries are without sodium, fat, cholesterol, and are a low-calorie organic product.

Green Tea:

Green tea helps shield our cells from any stress and catechins that are the dynamic mixes of green tea may expect a role in extending our metabolic rates.

Going for matcha green tea is a very smart thought since it includes crushed tea leaves, so it helps your energy levels.

Oats:

Oats are nutritious grains that various people consider to be a superfood. Among its clinical focal points, oats may improve heart prosperity, advance weight decrease, and help manage diabetes. Oats are rich in fiber. Dietary fiber is a sort of plant-based starch that the body cannot separate during osmosis. Fiber supports the absorption in preparing food adequately and helps food with going through the stomach related parcel. It may similarly have various favorable circumstances, for instance, engaging your body in weight decrease and hindering cardiovascular illness.

Dull Chocolate:

An unfathomable wellspring of flavonoids, chocolate can improve your wellbeing in different ways. A tad of faint chocolate is a mind-blowing answer for your sugar wants, and it underpins your endorphins and serotonin levels at the same time. The substances found in chocolate can similarly help fight stroke, coronary sickness, and hypertension.

Parsley:

High in chlorophyll, this can be a strong cell support. Parsley moreover has alpha-linolenic destructive structure, which is an omega-3 that can fight coronary sickness and joint torment. The luteolin in this spice may guarantee the wellbeing of your eyes too.

4.2 Optavia Breakfast Recipes

Following are some breakfast recipes rich in healthy nutrients that you can follow while being on the Optavia diet:

1) **Wild Blueberry Almond Hot Cereal Recipe**

Nutritional Value: 110 Calories

Preparation Time: 10 minutes

Cooking Time: 30 minutes

Serving: 2

Ingredients:
- Sliced almonds, two tbsp.
- Egg whites, six
- Almond extract, one tsp.
- Dry rolled oats, one cup
- Liquid stevia, twenty drops
- Coconut milk, half cup
- Wild blueberries, one cup

Instructions:
1. Combine all the ingredients together.
2. Pour the mixture into a baking dish, coated with coconut oil.
3. Add the one cup of frozen wild blueberries, on top.
4. Sprinkle the sliced almonds on top.
5. Set the dishes on a flat sheet pan.
6. Bake for twenty-five minutes in your preheated oven.
7. Once cooked, dish out and add fresh berries on top.
8. Your dish is ready to be served.

2) Lean and Green Egg Cup Recipe

Nutritional Value: 163 Calories

Preparation Time: 10 minutes

Cooking Time: 13 minutes

Serving: 4

Ingredients:

- Spinach, one cup
- Whole eggs, four
- Egg whites, six
- Salt to taste
- Pepper to taste
- Bacon slices, twelve
- Chopped green onions, half cup
- Chopped green chilies, two
- Cilantro, as required

Instructions:

1. In a large bowl, mix the whole eggs, egg whites, spinach, green onion, green chilies, salt and pepper together.
2. In a muffin tray spray a little grease and lay the bacon slices in each cup.
3. Bake for two to three minutes in a pre-heated oven.
4. Add the mixture into the muffin tray on top of the bacon slices.
5. Bake for ten minutes.
6. Add cilantro on top.
7. Your dish is ready to be served.

3) Egg Omelet with Avocado Slices Recipe

Nutritional Value: 176 Calories

Preparation Time: 5 minutes

Cooking Time: 10 minutes

Serving: 2

Ingredients:

- Sliced avocado, as required
- Turmeric powder, one tsp.
- Cherry tomatoes, four
- Spinach, one cup
- Eggs, four
- Salt to taste
- Pepper to taste
- Olive oil, half tsp.

Instructions:

1. Add the olive oil in a large pan and heat.
2. Mix the eggs, turmeric powder, salt and pepper in a bowl.
3. Add the egg mixture in the pan and cook until firm.
4. Add the spinach and cherry tomatoes on top of the omelet.
5. Place the avocado slices on top.
6. Your dish is ready to be served.

4) Cauliflower Breakfast Skillet Casserole Recipe

Nutritional Value: 137 Calories

Preparation Time: 10 minutes

Cooking Time: 40 minutes

Serving: 8

Ingredients:

- Small red onion, one

- Large eggs, twelve
- Milk, half cup
- Cauliflower florets, two cups
- Shredded mozzarella cheese, half cup
- Chicken sausage, half pound
- Italian herbs, one tsp.
- Shredded cheddar cheese, half cup
- Green onions, as required
- Salt to taste
- Pepper to taste

Instructions:
1. Add the onions in a pan and cook until soft.
2. Add the cauliflower florets into the pan and cook for a while.
3. Add the chicken sausage and cook for five minutes.
4. Add the Italian herbs, salt and pepper.
5. Add the milk and eggs in a bowl.
6. Add the cauliflower mixture into a baking dish and add the milk and egg mixture on top.
7. Add the cheese mixture on top and bake the dish for twenty-five minutes approximately.
8. Once the cheese is cooked and the color is changed into golden brown switch off the oven.
9. Add the green onions on top.
10. Your dish is ready to be served.

5) Feta and Spinach Egg Whites Recipe

Nutritional Value: 200 Calories

Preparation Time: 10 minutes

Cooking Time: 5 minutes

Serving: 2

Ingredients:

- Italian tomatoes, two
- Egg whites, three
- Crumbled feta cheese, half cup
- Salt to taste
- Pepper to taste
- Baby spinach, two cups
- Chopped onions, half cup
- Olive oil, half tsp.

Instructions:

1. Add the olive oil in a large pan and heat.
2. Mix the eggs, crumbled feta cheese, salt, and pepper in a bowl.
3. Add the egg mixture in the pan and cook until firm.
4. Add the spinach and cherry tomatoes on top of the omelet.
5. Your dish is ready to be served.

6) Fully Loaded Baked Egg Casserole Recipe

Nutritional Value: 172 Calories

Preparation Time: 20 minutes

Cooking Time: 40 minutes

Serving: 6

Ingredients:

- Whole milk, half cup
- Eggs, twelve
- Garlic powder, one tsp.
- Shredded cheddar cheese, one cup
- Salt to taste
- Pepper to taste
- Sausage rolls, one pound
- Smoked bacon, half pound
- Frozen hash browns, one package

Instructions:

1. In a pan add the sausages, and bacon.
2. Cook the meat very nicely.
3. Add the garlic powder, salt and pepper.
4. Mix the whole milk and eggs.
5. Add the meat mixture in a baking dish.
6. Add the frozen hash browns on top and then pour in the egg and milk mixture.
7. In the end,
8. add the cheese and bake for thirty minutes.
9. When the cheese turns golden brown in color, take it out from the oven.
10. Your dish is ready to be served.

7) Spinach and Egg White Omelet Recipe

Nutritional Value: 70 Calories

Preparation Time: 5 minutes

Cooking Time: 5 minutes

Serving: 2

Ingredients:
- Salt to taste
- Pepper to taste
- Spinach, two cups
- Egg whites, six

Instructions:
1. Add the olive oil in a large pan and heat.
2. Mix the eggs, salt, and pepper in a bowl.
3. Add the egg mixture in the pan and cook until firm.
4. Add the spinach on top of the omelet.
5. Your dish is ready to be served.

8) Cloud Bread Recipe

Nutritional Value: 36 Calories

Preparation Time: 10 minutes

Cooking Time: 15 minutes

Serving: 4-6

Ingredients:
- Cream of tartar, half tsp.
- Sea salt, as required
- Garlic powder, half tsp.
- Low fat cream cheese, two ounces

- Eggs, four
- Italian herb, one tsp.

Instructions:
1. In a bowl separate the egg whites and egg yolks.
2. Place the whites in a stand mixer with a whip attachment.
3. Add the cream of tartar and beat on high until the froth turns into firm peaks.
4. Place the cream cheese in the empty stand mixing bowl.
5. Then add the egg yolks one at a time to incorporate.
6. Scrape the bowl and beat until the mixture is completely smooth.
7. Then, beat in the Italian seasoning, salt, and garlic powder.
8. Gently fold the firm meringue into the yolk mixture.
9. Spoon some portions of the foam onto the baking sheets.
10. Make sure to leave space around each circle.
11. Bake for fifteen minutes.
12. Once the bread reaches the golden-brown color remove from the oven.
13. Your dish is ready to be served.

9) Cauliflower Waffles Recipe

Nutritional Value: 190 Calories

Preparation Time: 5 minutes

Cooking Time: 10 minutes

Serving: 3

Ingredients:
- Flour, two tbsp.
- Eggs, two
- Grated cauliflower, two cups
- Onion powder, two tsp.
- Oregano, half tsp.
- Salt to taste
- Pepper to taste
- Paprika, two tsp.
- Shredded mozzarella cheese, two cups

Instructions:
1. Preheat the waffle iron.
2. Transfer the cauliflower to a bowl, and then add the cheese, eggs, flour, paprika, onion powder, oregano, salt and pepper.
3. Mix together until well-blended.
4. Spray the waffle maker with non-stick spray.
5. Add about one cup of the cauliflower mixture to the pre-heated waffle iron.
6. Cook for six minutes.
7. Remove the cauliflower waffle from the iron.
8. Your dish is ready to be served.

10) Cauliflower Tortillas Recipe

Nutritional Value: 56 Calories

Preparation Time: 10 minutes

Cooking Time: 10 minutes

Serving: 4

Ingredients:

- Salt and pepper, to taste
- Vegetable oil, four tbsp.
- Cilantro, as required
- Ground cauliflower, two cups
- Eggs, two

Instructions:

1. Mix all the above ingredients together in a bowl.
2. Add vegetable oil into the pan.
3. Add cauliflower mixture and cook for ten minutes.
4. Cook until golden brown from both sides.
5. Your dish is ready to be served.

11) Ham and Vegetable Omelet Recipe

Nutritional Value: 162 Calories

Preparation Time: 20 minutes

Cooking Time: 5 minutes

Serving: 2

Ingredients:

- Cooked lean ham, half cup
- Red bell pepper, half cup
- Cheddar cheese, half cup

- Green bell pepper, half cup
- Yellow onion, one
- Eggs, four
- Vegetable oil, one tsp.

Instructions:
1. Mix all the above ingredients together in a bowl.
2. Add vegetable oil into the pan.
3. Add mixed vegetables and cook for ten minutes.
4. Add the cooked ham into the mixture.
5. Cook until golden brown from both sides.
6. Your dish is ready to be served.

12) Stuffed Biscuit Waffles Recipe

Nutritional Value: 152 Calories

Preparation Time: 10 minutes

Cooking Time: 15 minutes

Serving: 8

Ingredients:
- Salt to taste
- Pepper to taste
- Shredded cheddar cheese, half cup
- Milk, one tbsp.
- Eggs, three
- Refrigerated biscuit dough, one tube

Instructions:

1. Heat a medium non-stick skillet over medium low heat.
2. Crack the eggs into a medium bowl and whisk together with the milk.
3. Scramble the eggs until just slightly wet.
4. Stir in the cheese and remove from the heat.
5. Heat the waffle iron and spray with non-stick cooking spray.
6. Stuff the biscuits with the eggs and press the edges to seal the eggs inside.
7. Place a biscuit in the waffle iron and gently close the lid.
8. Do not press it fully closed.
9. Let it cook for one minute.
10. After one minute, fully close the waffle iron and continue cooking for two more minutes.
11. Your dish is ready to be served.

13) Vanilla Protein Crepes Recipe

Nutritional Value: 210 Calories

Preparation Time: 10 minutes

Cooking Time: 10 minutes

Serving: 6

Ingredients:

- Pumpkin pie spice, a quarter tsp.
- Coconut oil, half tsp.
- Gluten free flour, one cup
- Water, a quarter cup

- Vanilla essence, one tsp.
- Eggs, two
- Protein vanilla shake, one cup
- Salt, a pinch
- Pumpkin puree, three tbsp.
- Apple, one
- Brown sugar, three tbsp.

Instructions:
1. In a large bowl, mix the flour, eggs, protein shake, water, and salt.
2. Mix till batter is creamy and lump-free.
3. Then whisk in the melted coconut oil.
4. Place a pan over medium heat and grease it with coconut oil.
5. Add a ladle-full of batter to pan and twirl pan around so the batter coats the bottom of pan in a thin layer.
6. Flip and let cook about 30 seconds and transfer to a plate.
7. Add coconut oil to the same pan and add in the apple, coconut sugar, salt, pumpkin puree, vanilla and pumpkin pie spice.
8. Let it cook until the apple starts softening.
9. Place a couple of tablespoons of batter in each crepe.
10. Your dish is ready to be served.

14) Golden Chocolate Chip Pancakes Recipe

Nutritional Value: 161 Calories

Preparation Time: 10 minutes

Cooking Time: 5 minutes

Serving: 8

Ingredients:
- Eggs, two
- Sugar, two tbsp.
- Baking powder, three tsp.
- Milk, one cup
- Chocolate chips, half cup
- Oil, three tsp.
- All-purpose flour, two cups
- Salt, a pinch

Instructions:
1. In a bowl whisk together all-purpose flour, sugar, salt and baking powder.
2. In another bowl whisk together oil, eggs and milk.
3. Transfer wet ingredients to dry, keep mixing till well combined but do not overmix.
4. Fold in the chocolate chips and let the batter sit for five to ten minutes.
5. Heat a pan or skillet on medium heat, melt little butter and spread it all over.
6. Pour a ladle full of batter on to the pan.

7. Cook for a minute or two and flip the pancake when you see small bubbles on the surface.
8. Cook the other side for two to four minutes.
9. The pancake is ready when light golden brown in color.
10. Your dish is ready to be served.

15) Old Fashioned Maple and Brown Sugar Oatmeal Recipe

Nutritional Value: 120 Calories

Preparation Time: 10 minutes

Cooking Time: 15 minutes

Serving: 2

Ingredients:

- Rolled oats, one cup
- Maple syrup, one tbsp.
- Milk, two cups
- Brown sugar, two tsp.

Instructions:

1. Mix all ingredients in a saucepan.
2. Bring to a boil and reduce to medium heat stirring frequently.
3. Cook for five minutes until milk is absorbed.
4. Remove from heat and cool for several minutes.
5. Your dish is ready to be served.

16) Orchard Apple and Cinnamon Spiced Oatmeal Recipe

Nutritional Value: 196 Calories

Preparation Time: 15 minutes

Cooking Time: 40 minutes

Serving: 6

Ingredients:

- Vanilla extract, one tsp.
- Oats, two cups
- Sea salt, half tsp.
- Cinnamon, one tsp.
- Ground flaxseed, one tbsp.
- Coconut oil, one tsp.
- Diced apple, one
- Baking powder, one tsp.
- Milk, two cups
- Raisins, half cup
- Maple syrup, half cup
- Apple sauce, half cup

Instructions:

1. In a large bowl, mix together all the ingredients.
2. Fold everything effectively.
3. Fold in raisins and the diced apples.
4. Pour mixture into prepared baking dish.
5. Bake for forty minutes or until the center has set and a toothpick comes out clean.
6. Allow baked oatmeal to cool just a bit before serving.
7. Your dish is ready to be served.

17) Red Berry Crunchy O's Cereal Recipe

Nutritional Value: 110 Calories

Preparation Time: 10 minutes

Cooking Time: 5 minutes

Serving: 2

Ingredients:

- Whole milk, two cups
- Red berry Crunchy O's cereals, two cups
- Fresh red berries, as required
- Sugar, two tbsp.

Instructions:

1. Add the sugar into the milk and let it boil until the sugar dissolves properly.
2. Add the hot milk into the cereals.
3. Add fresh red berries on top.
4. Your dish is ready to be served.

18) Spinach and Egg Breakfast Wrap Recipe

Nutritional Value: 210 Calories

Preparation Time: 10 minutes

Cooking Time: 5 minutes

Serving: 4

Ingredients:

- Corn tortillas, four
- Pepper jack cheese, four ounces
- Salt, half tsp.
- Egg whites, four

- Avocado, one
- Baby spinach, one cup
- Whole eggs, four

Instructions:

1. Spray a nonstick skillet over medium-high heat.
2. Add spinach and cook, stirring, until wilted for two minutes.
3. Whisk together eggs and egg whites in a small bowl.
4. Add eggs to skillet and cook, stirring, until cooked through for three to four minutes.
5. Season with salt and pepper.
6. Place a quarter of the egg mixture in the center of each corn tortilla.
7. Add the cheese on top.
8. Top with the slices of avocado and fold it.
9. Your dish is ready to be served.

19) Lean Luxurious Eggs Recipe

Nutritional Value: 110 Calories

Preparation Time: 10 minutes

Cooking Time: 30 minutes

Serving: 2

Ingredients:

- Crushed garlic, one
- Salt to taste
- Pepper to taste
- Eggs, four

- Nutmeg, half tsp.
- Butter, one tbsp.
- Sour cream, one tbsp.
- Parsley, as required

Instructions:
1. Peel and crush the garlic.
2. Break the eggs into a large bowl, whisk until light and frothy.
3. Season well with salt and pepper.
4. Stir in the nutmeg.
5. Melt the butter over a low heat in a small heavy saucepan.
6. Add the garlic and cook gently for about one minute.
7. Add the eggs to the pan, stir rapidly with a fork for three to four minutes or until almost scrambled.
8. Stir in the cream and parsley.
9. Remove from heat and continue to stir until eggs are just set.
10. Your dish is ready to be served.

20) Egg Roll in a Bowl Recipe

Nutritional Value: 220 Calories

Preparation Time: 5 minutes

Cooking Time: 15 minutes

Serving: 4

Ingredients:
- Green onions, four
- Cilantro, as required

- Sesame seeds, as required
- Garlic cloves, four
- Ground pork, one pound
- Soy sauce, three tbsp.
- Ginger, two tsp.
- Sesame oil, one tsp.
- Coleslaw mix, one pound

Instructions:
1. Brown the ground pork in a pan until no pink color remains.
2. Remove the fat from the cooked pork.
3. Add the whites of the green onions, ginger, garlic, and coleslaw mix.
4. Cook until slaw is tender for approximately five minutes.
5. Stir in the soy sauce and sesame oil and keep mixing until soy sauce is evenly distributed.
6. Add the cilantro and sesame seeds on top.
7. Your dish is ready to be served.

4.3 Lunch Recipes

Following are some lunch recipes rich in healthy nutrients that you can follow while being on the Optavia diet:

1) Rolled Garlic Creamy Smashed Potato Recipe

Nutritional Value: 139 Calories

Preparation Time: 20 minutes

Cooking Time: 30 minutes

Serving: 10

Ingredients:
- Crushed garlic, six
- Kosher salt, two tbsp.
- Half and half, two cups
- Grated parmesan cheese, one cup
- Russet potatoes, four pounds

Instructions:
1. Peel and dice potatoes, making sure all are relatively of the same size.
2. Place in a large saucepan, add the salt, and cover with water.
3. Bring to a boil over medium-high heat and then reduce heat to maintain a rolling boil.
4. Cook until potatoes fall apart when poked with a fork.
5. Heat the half-and-half and the garlic in a medium saucepan over medium heat until simmering.
6. Remove from heat and set aside.
7. Remove the potatoes from the heat and drain off the water.
8. Mash and add the garlic-cream mixture and parmesan.
9. Let it cook for five minutes so that mixture thickens.
10. Your dish is ready to be served.

2) Grilled Steak Fajita Bowl Recipe

Nutritional Value: 360 Calories

Preparation Time: 15 minutes

Cooking Time: 20 minutes

Serving: 4

Ingredients:

- Yellow peppers, two
- Red peppers, two
- Ground cumin, two tsp.
- Vegetable oil, three tbsp.
- Yellow onions, two
- Cooked black beans, two cups
- Smoked paprika, two tsp.
- Flank steak, two pounds
- Salt, one tsp.
- Mexican oregano, one tbsp.
- Ground black pepper, one tsp.
- Chili powder, two tsp.
- Avocados, two
- Orange zest, two
- Lime zest, two
- Cilantro, half cup
- Orange juice, one cup
- Lime juice, half cup
- Green onions, one

- Garlic powder, one tsp.
- White wine vinegar, half cup
- Soy sauce, two tbsp.

Instructions:
1. To a blender or food processor add the all the liquid and zesty ingredients into it.
2. Blend it until a smooth texture is formed.
3. To large zip lock bag or container with a lid, add the steak and pour the mixture over.
4. Seal and refrigerate for at least two hours.
5. Remove steak from the mixture and let it cool down to the room temperature.
6. To a small bowl add the chili powder, cumin, salt and pepper.
7. Mix in the oil as well.
8. Add the peppers and onions to a bowl and pour over the oil and spices.
9. When the grill is hot, add the steak. Grill for five to seven minutes.
10. Remove from the grill to a cutting board and allow to rest.
11. Add the peppers and onions to the grill and keep cooking them for five minutes.
12. Slice the steak piece.
13. Arrange all the things in a bowl.
14. Your dish is ready to be served.

3) Vegan Herb Crusted Tofu Recipe

Nutritional Value: 150 Calories

Preparation Time: 10 minutes

Cooking Time: 40 minutes

Serving: 6

Ingredients:
- Smoked paprika, half tsp.
- Salt to taste
- Pepper to taste
- Nutritional yeast, half cup
- Olive oil two tbsp.
- Quinoa flour, half cup
- Dried sage, one tbsp.
- Italian seasoning, one tbsp.
- Tofu, two blocks
- Dried garlic, one tbsp.

Instructions:
1. Cut the tofu into small cubes.
2. In a bowl, whisk together all the dry ingredients.
3. Add the olive oil in a small bowl.
4. First, coat a tofu steak in oil.
5. Then, place the tofu in the bowl of the dry ingredients and coat the tofu with the dry mixture.
6. Keep the cubes on a baking sheet.
7. When ready to bake, place the baking sheet in the oven.
8. Bake for fifteen minutes approximately.

9. Your dish is ready to be served.

4) Crab Cakes Recipe

Nutritional Value: 120 Calories

Preparation Time: 10 minutes

Cooking Time: 20 minutes

Serving: 4

Ingredients:
- Chopped parsley, two tbsp.
- Canola oil, as required
- Worcestershire sauce, one tbsp.
- Crabmeat, one pound
- Large egg, one
- Hot sauce, one tbsp.
- Panko bread crumbs, one cup
- Mayonnaise, half cup
- Salt to taste
- Pepper to taste
- Dijon mustard, two tbsp.

Instructions:
1. In a large bowl, add together the Worcestershire sauce, hot sauce, egg, Dijon mustard, mayonnaise, pepper and salt.
2. In another bowl, add the crab meat, parsley and panko.
3. Mix both the mixtures together.
4. Roll the mixture into small balls.
5. In a large pan, add the oil.

6. Cook for five minutes.
7. Your dish is ready to be served.

5) Kung Pao Chicken Recipe

Nutritional Value: 380 Calories

Preparation Time: 10 minutes

Cooking Time: 10 minutes

Serving: 6

Ingredients:

- Soy sauce, two tbsp.
- Sugar, two tbsp.
- Chicken one pound
- Baking soda, one tsp.
- Cornstarch, one tsp.
- Chicken stock, half cup
- Hoisin sauce, one tsp.
- Chinese black vinegar, two tbsp.
- Garlic, one tbsp.
- Peanuts, half cup
- Sesame oil, two tsp.
- Sichuan pepper, one tbsp.
- Red bell pepper, one
- Green bell pepper, one
- Dried chilies, eight
- Green onions, half cup

Instructions:
1. Combine all ingredients for the chicken in a small bowl.
2. Let it rest for ten minutes approximately.
3. Whisk sauce ingredients together until sugar dissolves.
4. Add two tablespoons of cooking oil, allow to heat up, and then add marinated chicken.
5. Fry chicken for approximately four minutes while mixing, until edges are browned.
6. Stir in garlic, ginger, chili diced peppers and Sichuan peppercorns and let it cook for one minute.
7. Give the prepared sauce a mix, then pour it into the pan and bring it to a boil while stirring.
8. Once it begins to thicken slightly, add chicken back into the pan and mix all of the ingredients through the sauce until the chicken is evenly coated and sauce has thickened.
9. Stir in green onions, peanuts and sesame oil.
10. Toss well and continue to cook for further two minutes.
11. Your dish is ready to be served.

6) Tuscan Gateway Baked Chicken Recipe

Nutritional Value: 280 Calories

Preparation Time: 10 minutes

Cooking Time: 50 minutes

Serving: 6

Ingredients:
- Fresh rosemary, two sprigs
- Olive oil, two tbsp.
- White wine, one cup

- Onion, one
- Salt to taste
- Pepper to taste
- Chicken, four pounds
- Lemon zest, half cup
- Chicken stock, one cup

Instructions:
1. Mix all the ingredients together.
2. Cover the chicken with an aluminum foil.
3. Add the chicken as a whole into the oven and let it bake for forty minutes.
4. Now, remove the aluminum foil and let the chicken broil for ten minutes in the oven until it gains its yummy golden-brown color.
5. Once done, take out from the oven.
6. Your dish is ready to be served.

7) Mushroom Bun Sliders Recipe

Nutritional Value: 137 Calories

Preparation Time: 10 minutes

Cooking Time: 15 minutes

Serving: 4

Ingredients:
- Vegan butter, two tbsp.
- Olive oil, one tbsp.
- Salt to taste
- Portobello Mushrooms, twelve

- Slider buns, twelve
- Pepper to taste
- Italian seasoning, one tsp.

Instructions:
1. Heat the butter and oil in a medium sauté pan on medium high heat.
2. When the butter and oil mixture is hot and bubbly, use a spatula and spread evenly in the pan, add the mushrooms.
3. Sprinkle the Italian seasoning and salt and pepper on the mushrooms and cook for approximately five minutes then flip them over.
4. Cook for another five minutes or until the mushrooms are soft.
5. Add the mushroom on a bun.
6. Add any sauce you want.
7. Your dish is ready to be served.

8) Personal Portobello Mushroom Pizza Recipe

Nutritional Value: 210 Calories

Preparation Time: 10 minutes

Cooking Time: 25 minutes

Serving: 4

Ingredients:
- Portobello mushrooms, four
- Vegan gouda cheese, a quarter cup
- Broccoli, half cup
- Minced garlic, one

- Olive oil, two tbsp.
- Kalamata olives, six
- Fresh basil, three
- Salt to taste
- Pepper to taste
- Dried Italian seasoning, one tsp.

Instructions:

1. Cut the stems off the broccoli, so there are just florets left.
2. Bring a pot of water to a boil, add the broccoli florets.
3. Then, cook for six minutes.
4. In a small bowl, mix together pizza sauce, garlic, Italian seasoning, salt, pepper, and fresh chopped basil.
5. De-stem the mushroom, and then drizzle about half a tablespoon of the olive oil over each mushroom, followed by the garlic sprinkled over top.
6. Cook, stem side down, for about five to ten minutes.
7. Flip mushrooms over; pat any access water with paper towel.
8. Then, add a couple of spoonsful of pizza sauce, followed by the broccoli florets, a couple of slices of Kalamata olives, and some crumbled vegan Gouda cheese.
9. Turn oven to high broil and cook Portobello mushroom pizzas for three to five minutes.
10. Your dish is ready to be served.

9) Taco Stuffed Zucchini Boats Recipe

Nutritional Value: 261 Calories

Preparation Time: 15 minutes

Cooking Time: 20 minutes

Serving: 6

Ingredients:
- Ground cumin, one tsp.
- Chili powder, one tsp.
- Onion powder, one tsp.
- Tomato sauce, four ounces
- Zucchini, three
- Dried oregano, one tsp.
- Ground beef, one pound
- Salt to taste
- Black pepper to taste
- Mexican cheese, one cup
- Paprika, one tsp.
- Water, a quarter cup
- Avocado, as required
- Olives, as required
- Cilantro, as required

Instructions:
1. Trim the ends off zucchini.
2. Cut zucchini in half lengthwise and scoop out pulp.
3. Line up the zucchini in a baking dish.

4. Chop the pulp up and set aside.
5. In a medium sized pan add ground beef until no longer pink.
6. Drain the excess grease.
7. Add the reserved zucchini pulp and the chili powder, garlic powder, garlic powder, onion powder, dried oregano, paprika, cumin and salt and pepper to the ground beef.
8. Add the tomato sauce and water and combine.
9. Fill the zucchini boats evenly with the taco mixture.
10. Top with shredded cheddar cheese.
11. Bake uncovered for about twenty minutes or until zucchini is tender.
12. Remove from oven and top with favorite toppings.
13. Your dish is ready to be served.

10) Roasted Cauliflower White Cheddar Soup Recipe

Nutritional Value: 260 Calories

Preparation Time: 10 minutes

Cooking Time: 30 minutes

Serving: 4

Ingredients:
- Olive oil, two tbsp.
- Sugar, half tsp.
- Milk, three cups
- Butter, three tbsp.
- Salt to taste

- Pepper to taste
- Heavy cream, half cup
- Dried thyme, half tsp.
- All-purpose flour, two tbsp.
- Yellow onion, one
- Cheddar cheese, one cup
- Bay leaf, one
- Parmesan cheese, half cup
- Dried parsley, one tsp.
- Chicken broth, one cup
- Cauliflower, one large
- Minced garlic, one

Instructions:
1. Keep cauliflower on baking sheet, drizzle with olive oil and toss to evenly coat, then spread into an even layer and season lightly with salt and pepper.
2. Bake in preheated oven until golden.
3. In a large pot, melt butter over medium heat.
4. Add in onion and sauté until soft.
5. Add in flour and cook, stirring constantly for one and a half minute, adding in garlic during last thirty seconds of cooking.
6. While whisking, slowly pour in milk followed by chicken broth and cream.
7. Add in parsley, thyme, bay leaf, sugar, roasted cauliflower and season soup with salt and pepper.

8. Remove from heat and stir in sharp white cheddar and parmesan cheese.
9. Garnish with the remaining cheese.
10. Your dish is ready to be served.

11) Chicken Chili Recipe

Nutritional Value: 110 Calories

Preparation Time: 15 minutes

Cooking Time: 60 minutes

Serving: 6

Ingredients:
- Chili powder, one tsp.
- Yellow bell peppers, two
- Olive oil, two tbsp.
- Red bell peppers, two
- Kosher salt, as required
- Yellow onions, three cups
- Cayenne pepper, one tsp.
- Dried red pepper flakes, one tsp.
- Tomatoes, two
- Ground cumin, one tsp.
- Breast chicken, four
- Fresh basil leaves, four

Instructions:

1. Cook the onions in the oil over medium-low heat for ten minutes, until soft.
2. Add the garlic and cook for an additional minute.
3. Add the bell peppers, chili powder, cumin, red pepper flakes, cayenne, and salt. Crush the tomatoes by hand or in batches in a food processor fitted with a steel blade.
4. Add to the pot with the basil.
5. Bring to a boil, then reduce the heat and let it cook uncovered, for thirty minutes.
6. Rub the chicken breasts with olive oil and place them on a baking sheet.
7. Sprinkle generously with salt and pepper.
8. Roast the chicken for thirty minutes, until just cooked.
9. Separate the meat from the bones and skin and cut it into medium sized chunks.
10. Add to the chili and let it cook.
11. Your dish is ready to be served.

12) Chicken and Shrimp Gumbo Recipe

Nutritional Value: 210 Calories

Preparation Time: 20 minutes

Cooking Time: 30 minutes

Serving: 8

Ingredients:
- Red wine vinegar, one tbsp.
- Precooked brown rice, three cups
- Ground red pepper, two teaspoons
- Chicken stock, four cups
- Canola oil, six tbsp.
- All-purpose flour, half cup
- Frozen okra, three cups
- Chopped onion, two cups
- Chicken thigh, two pounds
- Celery, one cup
- Water, two cups
- Chopped garlic, five tsp.
- White wine, one cup
- Tomatoes, one can
- Shrimp, one pound
- Green onions, one cup

Instructions:
1. Reduce heat to medium-low.
2. Add remaining five tablespoons oil to pan.
3. Stir in the flour and cook for twenty minutes.
4. Whisk until the color is similar to the melted semi-sweet chocolate is attained.
5. Mix in the okra.

6. Increase heat to medium-high and cook for three minutes.
7. Mix in the wine and cook for two minutes.
8. Add stock and bring to a boil.
9. Reduce the heat and simmer for fifteen minutes.
10. Add the chicken and shrimp for three minutes.
11. Stir in the vinegar, black pepper, and rice.
12. Cook for five more minutes.
13. Top with green onions.
14. Your dish is ready to be served.

13) Crock Pot Pineapple Salsa Chicken Recipe

Nutritional Value: 230 Calories

Preparation Time: 5 minutes

Cooking Time: 3 hours

Serving: 4

Ingredients:
- Chunky salsa, three cups
- Pineapple reserves, one and a half cup
- Fresh chicken breasts, three pounds
- Chicken stock, three cups

Instructions:
1. Mix all the ingredients in a large pan.

2. Keep it on the stove and let it cook for three hours straight.
3. After three hours switch off the stove.
4. Your dish is ready to be served.

14) Balsamic Rosemary Chicken Recipe

Nutritional Value: 297 Calories

Preparation Time: 5 minutes

Cooking Time: 40 minutes

Serving: 4

Ingredients:
- Minced garlic, four
- Brown sugar, two tbsp.
- Olive oil, two tbsp.
- Balsamic vinegar, half cup
- Tamari, three tbsp.
- Red pepper flakes, one tbsp.
- Chicken breast, two pounds
- Fresh minced rosemary, three tbsp.
- Salt to taste
- Black pepper to taste

Instructions:
1. In a bowl add the chicken.

2. In another bowl whisk together the sugar, garlic, pepper, pepper flakes, rosemary, vinegar, tamari and olive oil until smooth texture is attained.
3. Pour the marinade over the chicken and cover tightly with plastic wrap.
4. Refrigerate for one hour.
5. Grill the chicken for twenty minutes.
6. Allow the chicken to rest for a few minutes before serving or slicing.
7. If using a grill pan or outdoor grill, it would be a good idea to spray with olive oil spray before preheating.
8. Cut the chicken into fine slices.
9. Your dish is ready to be served.

15) Blackened Shrimp Lettuce Wraps Recipe

Nutritional Value: 187 Calories

Preparation Time: 15 minutes

Cooking Time: 20 minutes

Serving: 4

Ingredients:
- Lettuce leaves, as required
- Shrimp, two pounds
- Paprika, one tsp.
- Lime juice, one tbsp.
- Cumin powder, one tsp.

- Pepper, as required
- Salt, as required
- Coconut aminos, one tsp.
- Lime zest, one tsp.
- Olive oil, two tbsp.
- Oregano, one tsp.
- Garlic powder, one tsp.
- Onion powder, one tsp.
- Chopped cilantro, as required
- Avocado, as needed
- Jalapeno slices, as required
- Salsa, as required

Instructions:
1. In a large mixing bowl, whisk together the liquid ingredients.
2. Add the shrimp to the bowl and toss.
3. Pour contents of bowl into a reseal-able plastic bag.
4. Refrigerate for five minutes.
5. Heat a tablespoon of olive oil in a large pan over medium-high.
6. Once hot, add the shrimp in an even-layer.
7. Cook for three minutes on one side.
8. Flip each shrimp over.

9. Cook the other side for an additional three minutes or until the shrimps are no longer opaque and are cooked through.
10. Wrap the shrimp mixture in the lettuce leaves with your preferred toppings.
11. Your dish is ready to be served.

16) Cauliflower Bread Sticks Recipe

Nutritional Value: 47 Calories

Preparation Time: 10 minutes

Cooking Time: 20 minutes

Serving: 4

Ingredients:
- Egg whites, four
- Salt to taste
- Pepper to taste
- Marinara sauce, as required
- Mozzarella cheese, one cup
- Cauliflower, one large
- Olive oil, two tbsp.

Instructions:
1. Rinse the cauliflower, remove outer leaves and separate into florets with a paring knife.
2. Place the cauliflower florets in a food processor and process until grainy texture is formed.

3. Place in an ovenproof baking dish and bake for twenty minutes.
4. Remove the cooked cauliflower from the oven and transfer to a bowl.
5. Increase oven temperature to 450 degrees.
6. Transfer the cauliflower to a mixing bowl along with egg whites, half cup cheese, herb seasoning, black pepper, pinch of salt and mix to combine.
7. Transfer cauliflower mixture onto the baking sheet lined with unbleached parchment paper.
8. Bake for eighteen minutes, remove from the oven and top with remaining cheese.
9. Bake for another five minutes and then broil until cheese turns golden brown.
10. Cut into the twelve breadsticks and serve hot with warm marinara sauce.
11. Your dish is ready to be served.

17) Buffalo Cauliflower Wings Recipe

Nutritional Value: 172 Calories

Preparation Time: 10 minutes

Cooking Time: 30 minutes

Serving: 4

Ingredients:
- Water, half cup
- Paprika, one tsp.
- Garlic powder, one tsp.
- Ground pepper, to taste

- Salt, to taste
- Cumin powder, one tsp.
- Cauliflower, one large
- Milk, half cup
- Hot sauce, one cup
- Butter, one tbsp.
- All-purpose flour, one tbsp.

Instructions:
1. Line the baking sheet with parchment paper or grease very well with oil.
2. Preheat your oven to 400 degrees.
3. Wash and cut cauliflower head into bite-sized pieces.
4. Mix all the ingredients and spices in a medium mixing bowl.
5. Mix until the batter is thick and is able to coat the cauliflower without dripping.
6. Dip the cauliflower in the batter.
7. You can do this one by one or in batches.
8. Lay the cauliflower single layer on the baking sheet.
9. Bake for twenty minutes or until golden brown, flipping the florets over halfway through to get all sides golden brown and crispy.
10. In a small saucepan low heat, melt butter and mix in hot sauce.
11. Remove from the heat just as it starts to melt.

12. Once the cauliflower is done its first bake in the batter, remove them from the oven and put all the baked florets into a mixing bowl with the wing sauce and toss to coat evenly.
13. Place the cauliflower to the baking sheet and bake in the oven for another fifteen minutes or until it reaches its desired crispness.
14. Serve with ranch, blue cheese, or your favorite dipping sauce.
15. Your dish is ready to be served.

18) Peri-Peri Pork and Cauliflower Steaks Recipe

Nutritional Value: 310 Calories

Preparation Time: 10 minutes

Cooking Time: 25 minutes

Serving: 4

Ingredients:
- Olive oil, two tbsp.
- Red bell pepper, one
- Dried oregano, one tsp.
- Tomatoes, one
- Red wine vinegar, two tbsp.
- Smoked paprika, one tsp.
- Cauliflower, one
- Granulated sugar, two tbsp.

- Bay leaf, one
- Salt, to taste
- Black pepper, to taste
- Garlic cloves, five
- Red onion, one

Instructions:
1. Remove the leaves from the stem of cauliflower.
2. Leave the core intact.
3. Place cauliflower core side down and using a large knife, slice cauliflower into four half inch steaks from the center of cauliflower.
4. Arrange the cauliflower steaks on an oiled baking sheet with any broken florets.
5. Brush the cauliflower slices generously on both sides with olive oil, and sprinkle with salt and pepper, then roast in the oven for twenty minutes, until golden and cooked through.
6. You can flip the steaks halfway through cooking.
7. When the cauliflower steaks are done, remove from oven and transfer onto individual serving plates.
8. Combine all the ingredients in a blender or a food processor and process until all the ingredients are finely chopped and the mixture becomes a sauce.
9. Cook for twenty minutes.
10. Top each steak with some peri-peri sauce, micro greens, and a sprinkle of pine nuts.
11. Your dish is ready to be served.

19) Skinny BBQ Chicken Flatbread Pizza Recipe

Nutritional Value: 160 Calories

Preparation Time: 10 minutes

Cooking Time: 15 minutes

Serving: 4

Ingredients:
- Olive oil, two tbsp.
- Shredded BBQ chicken, one cup
- Red onion, half
- BBQ sauce, half cup
- Flatbread crust, one
- Mozzarella cheese, one cup
- Butter, four tbsp.

Instructions:
1. Preheat the oven to 350 degrees.
2. In a pan, melt butter and add onion slices.
3. Sauté until soft.
4. Spray or spread a small amount of olive oil over the top of your flatbread.
5. It does not need to be wet, just a little coat.
6. Spread BBQ sauce over the olive oil on the flatbread.

7. Add sautéed onions to the flatbread and the BBQ chicken.
8. Top with mozzarella cheese.
9. Bake in oven, directly on rack, for ten minutes, or until cheese is melted and bread is crispy.
10. Your dish is ready to be served.

20) Chicken Cacciatore Recipe

Nutritional Value: 310 Calories

Preparation Time: 10 minutes

Cooking Time: 40 minutes

Serving: 6

Ingredients:
- Roma tomatoes, one cup
- Minced garlic, two tbsp.
- Carrot, one large
- Yellow bell pepper, one
- Red wine, half cup
- Onion, one
- Chicken thighs, six
- Parsley, one tsp.
- Basil, one tsp.
- Dried oregano, one tsp.
- Salt to taste

- Pepper, as required
- Tomato paste, two tbsp.
- Red pepper flakes, half tsp.
- Black olives, half cup
- Thyme, one tsp.
- Red bell pepper, one
- Olive oil, two tbsp.

Instructions:
1. Season chicken with salt and pepper.
2. Heat the two tablespoons oil in a heavy cast iron pan.
3. Cook chicken on both sides until golden.
4. Remove from pan and set aside.
5. Add remaining oil to the pan.
6. Sauté the onion until transparent.
7. Add in garlic and cook until fragrant for about thirty seconds.
8. Add the peppers, carrot, mushrooms and herbs; cook for five minutes until vegetables begin to soften.
9. Pour in the wine, scraping up browned bits from the bottom of the pan.
10. Cook until wine is reduced for about two minutes.
11. Add crushed tomatoes, tomato paste, Roma tomatoes and pepper flakes.
12. Season with salt and pepper to your tastes.
13. Add the chicken pieces to the skillet and continue to cook over stove top.

14. Cook for ten minutes.

15. Your dish is ready to be served.

4.4 Dinner Recipes

Following are some dinner recipes rich in healthy nutrients that you can follow while being on the Optavia diet:

1) Grilled Stuffed Chicken Italiano Recipe

Nutritional Value: 164 Calories

Preparation Time: 12 minutes

Cooking Time: 13 minutes

Serving: 4

Ingredients:
- Baby spinach, twenty pieces
- Mozzarella cheese, one cup
- Chicken breasts, four
- Roasted red peppers, four
- Italian dressing, as required

Instructions:
1. Preheat the grill to medium high temperature.
2. Cut the chicken breasts.
3. Place about five baby spinach leaves in middle.

4. Put the roasted red pepper, and cheese on top of spinach.
5. Roll like a cigar, and put some toothpicks on ends to hold together well.
6. Grill for five minutes, turn and grill five more minutes.
7. If the chicken is done slice it up.
8. Your dish is ready to be served.

2) Pizza with Chicken and Tzatziki Recipe

Nutritional Value: 110 Calories

Preparation Time: 10 minutes

Cooking Time: 30 minutes

Serving: 2

Ingredients:
- Lemon juice, one tbsp.
- Kalamata olives, as required
- Feta cheese, a quarter cup
- Fresh dill, two tbsp.
- Oregano, one tsp.
- Greek pita bread, four
- Garlic, one
- Sun dried tomatoes, half cup
- Shredded chicken breast, one cup
- Artichoke hearts, half cup

- Cucumber, one
- Greek yoghurt, one cup
- Olive oil, one tbsp.

Instructions:

1. Add garlic, cucumber and dill to the bowl of a food processor fit with a metal blade and blend the ingredients.
2. Add yogurt, sour cream, lemon juice and dill and pulse to blend.
3. Add salt to taste.
4. Refrigerate for one hour.
5. Preheat the oven to 450 degrees.
6. Place the pita breads domed side down on a baking sheet covered with parchment paper.
7. Spread on each bread some of tzatziki, then top each with mozzarella cheese.
8. Layer the chicken breast, olives, tomatoes and artichoke hearts on top of the mozzarella then top with sprinkling of feta cheese and a sprinkle of oregano.
9. Place in oven and bake for ten minutes or until cheese is melted and feta cheese starts to turn golden.
10. Remove, garnish with fresh dill sprigs, red chili flakes and more feta if desired, cut into quarters.
11. Your dish is ready to be served.

3) Bruschetta Grilled Chicken Recipe

Nutritional Value: 140 Calories

Preparation Time: 20 minutes

Cooking Time: 30 minutes

Serving: 2

Ingredients:

- Italian seasoning, one tbsp.
- Chicken breasts, four
- Lemon juice, one tbsp.
- Garlic cloves, two
- Olive oil, four tbsp.
- Chopped basil, one tbsp.
- Mozzarella cheese, four slices
- Salt, to taste
- Black pepper, to taste
- Tomato mixture, half cup
- Dried oregano, half tsp.

Instructions:

1. In a small bowl, combine oil, lemon juice of half of the lemon, a teaspoon of salt, half a teaspoon pepper, and Italian seasoning as well as oregano.
2. Transfer to a large re-sealable bag along with chicken; seal and refrigerate for thirty minutes.
3. Heat the grill over medium-high then add chicken.

4. Grill until you see that the chicken is cooked properly.
5. Meanwhile, combine tomatoes, garlic, basil, and remaining lemon juice, and season with salt and pepper.
6. While chicken is still on grill, top each breast with a slice of mozzarella and cover until cheese is melted.
7. Top chicken with tomato mixture.
8. Your dish is ready to be served.

4) Roast Garlic Grilled Marinated Flank Steak Recipe

Nutritional Value: 290 Calories

Preparation Time: 5 minutes

Cooking Time: 20 minutes

Serving: 6

Ingredients:
- Flank steak, two pounds
- Olive oil, half cup
- Pepper, as required
- Salt, as required
- Garlic powder, one tsp.
- Lemon juice, one tbsp.
- Lemon zest, one tsp.
- Italian herb mix, two tbsp.

Instructions:

1. Season the steak with salt and pepper.
2. Add olive oil, herbs, lemon zest and juice, and diced garlic to a large bowl.
3. Heat the grill on medium high.
4. Remove steak from the bowl, and sprinkle with garlic powder.
5. Cook steak on very hot grill, flipping every five minutes.
6. For medium rare steak, the steak will cook for about ten minutes.
7. For a steak that is medium all the way to well done, cook the steak directly over the heat, flipping twice, for ten minutes.
8. Remove from grill when steak is done.
9. When steak has stayed for at least ten minutes, slice it up.
10. Your dish is ready to be served.

5) Shrimp and Cauliflower Grits Recipe

Nutritional Value: 110 Calories

Preparation Time: 10 minutes

Cooking Time: 30 minutes

Serving: 4

Ingredients:

- Milk, one cup
- Ground black pepper, as required

- Salt, as required
- Shrimp, two pounds
- Chopped parsley, half cup
- Cauliflower, one
- Minced garlic, one tsp.
- Cayenne pepper, a pinch
- Grated parmesan, half cup
- Unsalted butter, three tbsp.
- Lemon juice, two tbsp.

Instructions:
1. Add about half of the cauliflower in a food processor until the florets break down into finer pieces about the size of grains of rice.
2. Transfer to a medium saucepan, pulse the remaining cauliflower and add that to the pan too.
3. Add the milk, a tablespoon of the butter, half teaspoon salt and several grinds of pepper and bring to a simmer over medium-high heat.
4. Cook, mixing frequently, until the mixture is soft and smooth and looks like grits for ten minutes.
5. Remove from the heat, stir in the parmesan and adjust the seasoning with more salt and pepper.
6. Cover and keep warm.
7. Season the shrimp with salt and pepper.
8. Melt the remaining two tablespoons of butter in a large skillet over medium-high heat.

9. Add the shrimp, garlic and cayenne if using and cook, tossing, until the shrimps are pink and just cooked through.
10. Remove from the heat, add the parsley, lemon juice and a tablespoon of water and stir to coat the shrimp with the sauce.
11. Season with salt and pepper.
12. Divide the cauliflower grits among shallow bowls and top with the shrimp and sauce.
13. Your dish is ready to be served.

6) Rosemary and Garlic Beef Stew Recipe

Nutritional Value: 110 Calories

Preparation Time: 10 minutes

Cooking Time: 2 hours

Serving: 6

Ingredients:
- Beef broth, two cups
- Ground pepper, to taste
- Salt, as required
- Beef stew meat, two pounds
- Rosemary, two tsp.
- Tomato paste, two tbsp.
- Garlic, two
- Potatoes, three
- Onions, one

- Carrots, two
- Mushrooms, one and a half cup
- All-purpose flour, a quarter cup
- Butter, two tbsp.
- Oil, two tbsp.

Instructions:
1. Season the beef with salt and pepper.
2. Dredge the beef in flour.
3. Heat oil and butter in a large Dutch oven and add beef in two batches.
4. Brown the meat on either side, and remove it in a bowl with a slotted spoon.
5. Add garlic and onions to the pan and sauté for a few minutes.
6. Stir in the tomato paste and cook for another minute or two.
7. While the tomato paste is being cooked, pre-heat oven to 350 degrees.
8. Add beef, carrots, potatoes, mushrooms, thyme, rosemary, salt and pepper and pour in the beef broth.
9. Bring this to a boil and then transfer to the oven for two hours approximately.
10. Place it with mashed potatoes, bread or brown rice.
11. Your dish is ready to be served.

7) Swedish Meatballs with Zucchini Noodles Recipe

Nutritional Value: 216 Calories

Preparation Time: 10 minutes

Cooking Time: 20 minutes

Serving: 8

Ingredients:

- Almond flour, a quarter cup
- All spice half tsp.
- Worcestershire sauce, one tbsp.
- Nutmeg, a quarter tsp.
- Ground pork, one pound
- Ground beef, one pound
- Olive oil, two tbsp.
- Sour cream, half cup
- Salt, to taste
- Pepper, to taste
- Beef stock, one cup
- Heavy cream, half cup
- Zucchini, two
- Garlic salt, half tsp.

Instructions:

1. Add olive oil, salt and pepper over the zucchini and place it in the oven.

2. Shred the zucchini once it is done.
3. Heat a pan.
4. Sauté the onion in a little olive oil.
5. Add a little salt and cook until translucent.
6. Remove from heat and set aside to cool slightly.
7. In a large bowl, add the eggs, parsley, salt, pepper, garlic salt, almond flour, nutmeg, allspice, Worcestershire and onion.
8. Add the ground beef and pork and mix well.
9. Form the meatballs in small sizes.
10. Sauté the meatballs in olive oil until well-browned.
11. Remove the meatballs to a platter lined with paper towels as they are done.
12. Discard most of the fat from the skillet and return it to the heat.
13. Add the chicken stock to deglaze the pan, and then add the sour cream and heavy cream.
14. Add the meatballs back in and continue to simmer for twenty minutes or until sauce has thickened to your liking.
15. Mix the shredded zucchini and the mixture above.
16. Your dish is ready to be served.

8) Greek Chicken Burgers with Tzatziki Sauce Recipe

Nutritional Value: 110 Calories

Preparation Time: 15 minutes

Cooking Time: 15 minutes

Serving: 4

Ingredients:
- Greek yoghurt, half cup
- Ground chicken, one pound
- Cornstarch, one tbsp.
- Chopped garlic, two
- Salt to taste
- Pepper to taste
- Chopped fresh tomatoes, two
- Chopped onion, two tbsp.
- Chopped mint, two tbsp.
- Fresh spinach, four leaves
- Oregano leaves, one tsp.
- Cucumber, half cup
- Whole grain pita bread, four

Instructions:
1. Set oven control to broil.
2. Chop enough cucumber to equal half cup.
3. Stir in remaining sauce ingredients; refrigerate until ready to use.

4. In large bowl, mix chicken, spinach, olives, cornstarch, oregano, garlic, salt and pepper.
5. Shape into four oval patties.
6. On broiler pan, place patties.
7. Broil with tops about five inches from heat ten minutes, turning once, until thermometer inserted in center of burgers reads at least 170 degrees.
8. Place burgers in pita pocket halves.
9. Top each burger with tomato, cucumber slices and about three tablespoons sauce.
10. Your dish is ready to be served.

9) Baked Cod with Tomatoes and Feta Recipe

Nutritional Value: 147 Calories

Preparation Time: 10 minutes

Cooking Time: 30 minutes

Serving: 4

Ingredients:
- Crushed red pepper, a dash
- Kosher salt, two tsp.
- Olive oil, one tbsp.
- Chopped tomatoes, three
- White wine, a quarter cup
- Chopped onion, one
- Red wine vinegar, one tbsp.

- Oregano, two tsp.
- Cod filets, four
- Feta cheese, two ounces
- Black pepper, as required

Instructions:
1. Heat a large ovenproof skillet over medium heat.
2. Add the oil and swirl to coat.
3. Add the onion and sauté for five minutes or until tender.
4. Stir in the tomato, wine, a teaspoon oregano, vinegar, salt, black pepper, and crushed red pepper; bring to a simmer.
5. Cook for three minutes, mixing occasionally.
6. Sprinkle fish evenly with remaining salt.
7. Mix the fish in tomato mixture.
8. Bake at 400 degrees for fifteen minutes or until fish flakes easily when tested with a fork.
9. Sprinkle with remaining oregano, parsley, and feta.
10. Your dish is ready to be served.

10) Cheesy Chicken Cauliflower Skillet Recipe

Nutritional Value: 210 Calories

Preparation Time: 10 minutes

Cooking Time: 30 minutes

Serving: 4

Ingredients:
- Riced cauliflower, two cups
- Water, a quarter cup
- Canned black beans, one cup
- Frozen corn kernels, half cup
- Salsa, one cup
- Olive oil, one tbsp.
- Taco seasoning, three tbsp.
- Cheddar cheese, two ounces

Instructions:
1. Place the chicken breast cutlets in a gallon zip-top bag and add two tablespoons of the taco seasoning.
2. Seal the bag and toss to coat the chicken in the seasoning.
3. In a large sauté pan or walled skillet, bring the olive oil over medium heat.
4. Add the chicken in a single layer and cook on one side for five minutes.

5. Flip each piece and cook for an additional three minutes or until each piece is cooked through.
6. Transfer the chicken to a side plate and cover with aluminum foil to keep warm.
7. Add the cauliflower rice, salsa, water, the remaining tablespoon of taco seasoning, corn and black beans to the skillet and stir to combine.
8. Cover and cook over medium heat for five minutes.
9. Remove the lid to stir, cover and reduce heat to medium-low.
10. Continue to cook for another five minutes or until the cauliflower is softened.
11. Remove the lid, stir the contents and then sprinkle the cheese over the top.
12. Add the reserved chicken in a single layer on top of the cheese and replace the lid.
13. Turn off the burner and let the skillet stay, covered, for two minutes until the cheese is melted.
14. Your dish is ready to be served.

11) Seared Scallops in Creamy Garlic Sauce Recipe

Nutritional Value: 195 Calories

Preparation Time: 10 minutes

Cooking Time: 10 minutes

Serving: 4

Ingredients:
- Fresh parsley, three tbsp.
- Heavy cream, half cup
- Garlic cloves, four

- Butter, one tbsp.
- Salt to taste
- Pepper to taste
- Olive oil, two tbsp.
- White wine, half cup
- Red pepper flakes, half tsp.

Instructions:
1. In a medium sauce pan, over medium heat, add the butter and garlic.
2. Sauté for about two minutes or just right before the garlic begins to brown.
3. Deglaze with the wine, turn heat to medium and reduce until half of the liquid is gone.
4. Add the parsley, red pepper flakes, and cream.
5. Turn the heat to low and simmer until the cream thickens.
6. Rinse the scallops, pat with a paper towel until dry and season both sides with a little sea salt and pepper.
7. In a cast iron pan, over medium high heat, heat the butter and olive oil for a minute.
8. Add the scallops, be careful not to overcrowd the pan, and cook until opaque.
9. This will take about two minutes on each side depending on the size of scallop.
10. Pour the garlic cream sauce over the scallops.
11. Your dish is ready to be served.

12) Tropical Chicken Medley Recipe

Nutritional Value: 130 Calories

Preparation Time: 10 minutes

Cooking Time: 10 minutes

Serving: 2

Ingredients:
- Mango, one
- Pineapple juice, two tbsp.
- Black pepper, as required
- Avocado, one
- Ground cumin, half tsp.
- Apple cider vinegar, one tbsp.
- Jicama, one
- Cilantro leaves, as required
- Chili powder, one tsp.
- Serrano chili, one
- Chicken breast, two
- Pineapple, one cup
- Sea salt, as required

Instructions:
1. Grill the chicken breast pieces by adding olive oil, salt and pepper into it.
2. Once done, slice the chicken breast up nicely.

3. Mix the rest of the ingredients together.
4. Add the grilled chicken slices on top.
5. Your dish is ready to be served.

13) Cheeseburger Soup Recipe

Nutritional Value: 110 Calories

Preparation Time: 20 minutes

Cooking Time: 30 minutes

Serving: 4

Ingredients:
- Cheddar cheese, two cups
- Chicken broth, three cups
- All-purpose flour, a quarter cup
- Milk, one and a half cup
- Ground beef, half pound
- Shredded carrots, one cup
- Dried basil, one tsp.
- Chopped onion, one
- Dried parsley, one tsp.
- Celery, one cup
- Butter, four tbsp.
- Sour cream, a quarter cup

Instructions:
1. In a large pot, melt a tablespoon butter or margarine over medium heat.

2. Cook and stir vegetables and beef, until the beef is brown.
3. Stir in basil and parsley.
4. Add broth and potatoes.
5. Bring to a boil, and then simmer until potatoes are tender for about ten minutes.
6. Melt the remainder of butter and stir in flour.
7. Add the milk, stirring until smooth.
8. Gradually add milk mixture to the soup, stirring constantly.
9. Bring to a boil and reduce heat to simmer.
10. Stir in the cheese.
11. When the cheese is melted, add sour cream and heat through.
12. Dish out once it is done.
13. Your dish is ready to be served.

14) Lemon Garlic Oregano Chicken with Asparagus Recipe

Nutritional Value: 110 Calories

Preparation Time: 10 minutes

Cooking Time: 30 minutes

Serving: 2

Ingredients:
- Olive oil, two tbsp.
- Salt to taste

- Pepper, as required
- Minced garlic, two tbsp.
- Oregano, two tsp.
- Asparagus, one pound
- Mozzarella cheese, half cup
- Dried thyme, one tsp.
- Unsalted butter, three tbsp.
- Chicken breasts, two
- Parmesan cheese, a quarter cup
- Garlic powder, one tsp.
- Heavy cream, half cup
- Pasta, seven ounces
- Chicken breasts, two

Instructions:
1. In a large pot bring water to a boil and add the pasta.
2. Cook according to package directions.
3. Drain and set aside.
4. While the pasta is being cooked, heat olive oil in a large skillet over medium-high heat.
5. Add the chicken and season with salt, black pepper and oregano.
6. Cook for five minutes, stirring occasionally until browned and cooked through.
7. Add a teaspoon of minced garlic and cook for another minute, until fragrant. Transfer to plate and set aside.

8. Add butter to the same skillet and melt over medium high heat.
9. Add remaining minced garlic and asparagus and sauté for one minute, until just starting to turn bright green.
10. Whisk in the cream, lemon juice, lemon zest, garlic powder, oregano, parmesan, and mozzarella cheese.
11. Allow the sauce to thicken and cheese to melt.
12. Add the drained pasta and chicken back into the skillet.
13. Season with salt and black pepper to taste.
14. Mix to coat well until everything is heated through.
15. Sprinkle with more parmesan cheese, chopped parsley, and lemon slices.
16. Your dish is ready to be served.

15) Curry Crusted Salmon with Chili Braised Napa Cabbage Recipe

Nutritional Value: 110 Calories

Preparation Time: 10 minutes

Cooking Time: 30 minutes

Serving: 4

Ingredients:

- Grapeseed oil, two tbsp.
- Curry powder, two tsp.
- Basmati rice, one cup
- Fresh mint leaves, half cup
- Salt, to taste
- Pepper, to taste
- Carrots, one pound

- Napa cabbage, one pound
- Salmon filet, four

Instructions:
1. In a large saucepan, bring two cups water to a boil.
2. Add in the rice.
3. Season with salt and pepper, cover, and reduce heat to medium-low.
4. Cook until tender for thirty minutes.
5. Meanwhile, in a large bowl, combine cabbage, carrots, mint, lime juice, and oil; season with salt and pepper.
6. Heat broiler on medium high.
7. About ten minutes before rice is done cooking, place salmon on a foil-lined rimmed baking sheet.
8. Rub salmon with curry, and season with salt and pepper.
9. Broil until just cooked through for six to eight minutes.
10. Fluff rice with a fork and serve alongside salad and salmon.
11. Your dish is ready to be served.

16) Balsamic Garlic Roasted Green Beans and Mushrooms Recipe

Nutritional Value: 179 Calories

Preparation Time: 10 minutes

Cooking Time: 20 minutes

Serving: 6

Ingredients:

- Olive oil, two tbsp.
- Balsamic vinegar, one tbsp.
- Fresh green beans, one pound
- Salt, to taste
- Pepper, to taste
- Garlic cloves, eight
- Mushrooms, ten ounces

Instructions:

1. Preheat oven to 450 degrees.
2. Line a large rimmed baking sheet with foil and spray with non-stick cooking spray.
3. Spread green beans, mushrooms and garlic in an even layer on the prepared baking sheet.
4. In a small bowl, whisk together olive oil and balsamic vinegar.
5. Drizzle over vegetables in pan and toss to coat evenly.
6. Season with salt and pepper, to taste.
7. Bake for twenty minutes, or until beans are tender-crisp.
8. Your dish is ready to be served.

17) Zucchini Ravioli Recipe

Nutritional Value: 110 Calories

Preparation Time: 15 minutes

Cooking Time: 60 minutes

Serving: 4

Ingredients:
- Marinara sauce, two cups
- Ricotta, two cups
- Zucchini, four
- Large egg, one
- Olive oil, two tbsp.
- Minced garlic, one
- Sliced basil, a quarter cup
- Shredded mozzarella cheese, half cup
- Ground black pepper, as required
- Grated parmesan cheese, half cup
- Kosher salt, as required
- Ravioli pasta, one pack

Instructions:
1. Preheat oven to 375 degrees.
2. Grease a large baking dish with olive oil.
3. Slice two sides of each zucchini lengthwise to create two flat sides.

4. Using a vegetable peeler, slice each zucchini into thin flat strips, peeling until you reach the center.
5. In a medium bowl, combine ricotta, parmesan, egg, two tablespoons basil, garlic, and season with salt and pepper.
6. Lay two strips of zucchini noodles so that they overlap lengthwise.
7. Lay two more noodles on top, perpendicular to the first strips.
8. Spoon about a tablespoon of filling in the center of the zucchini.
9. Bring the ends of the strips together to fold over the center, working on one side at a time.
10. Turn ravioli over and place in the baking dish seam-side down.
11. Repeat with remaining zucchini and filling.
12. Pour marinara around zucchini and top ravioli with mozzarella.
13. Bake for thirty minutes.
14. Top with remaining basil and parmesan cheese.
15. Your dish is ready to be served.

18) Italian Frittata Recipe

Nutritional Value: 211 Calories

Preparation Time: 25 minutes

Cooking Time: 25 minutes

Serving: 6

Ingredients:

- Eggs, six
- Diced salami, half cup
- Milk, half cup
- Cherry tomatoes, half cup
- Minced garlic, one
- Mushrooms, one can
- Onion powder, one tsp.
- Mozzarella cheese, one cup
- Salt, to taste
- Parmesan cheese, one cup
- Pepper, to taste
- Dried basil, one tsp.
- Artichokes, half cup

Instructions:

1. Preheat oven to 425 degrees.
2. Grease a shallow baking dish.
3. Heat a skillet over medium heat; cook and stir salami, artichokes, tomatoes, and mushrooms until heated through for five minutes.
4. Transfer salami mixture to baking dish.
5. Whisk eggs, milk, green onions, garlic, basil, onion powder, salt, and black pepper in a large bowl.
6. Pour the eggs over salami mixture.
7. Sprinkle with mozzarella cheese and Parmesan cheese.

8. Bake until eggs are set and cheese melts for about twenty minutes.
9. Your dish is ready to be served.

19) Grilled Shrimp Scampi Recipe

Nutritional Value: 173 Calories

Preparation Time: 30 minutes

Cooking Time: 6 minutes

Serving: 4

Ingredients:
- Minced garlic, one tbsp.
- Shrimps, two pounds
- Olive oil, a quarter cup
- Fresh parsley, three tbsp.
- Ground black pepper, as required
- Salt, to taste
- Lemon juice, a quarter cup

Instructions:
1. In a large bowl, stir together the olive oil, lemon juice, parsley, garlic, and black pepper.
2. Season with crushed red pepper, if desired.
3. Add shrimps, and toss to coat.
4. Marinate in the refrigerator for thirty minutes.
5. Preheat grill on high heat.
6. Thread shrimps onto skewers, piercing once near the tail and once near the head.

7. Lightly oil grill grate.
8. Grill for five minutes.
9. Your dish is ready to be served.

20) Broiled Grilled Burger with Lettuce Wraps Recipe

Nutritional Value: 110 Calories

Preparation Time: 15 minutes

Cooking Time: 10 minutes

Serving: 2

Ingredients:

- Red onion, one
- American cheese, six slices
- Seasoned salt, half tsp.
- Light mayonnaise, a quarter cup
- Roman lettuce, two
- Black pepper, one tsp.
- Ground beef, two pounds
- Ketchup, three tbsp.
- Tomatoes, two
- Dill pickle relish, one tbsp.

Instructions:

1. Heat a grill or skillet on medium heat.
2. In a large bowl, mix together ground beef, seasoned salt, pepper and oregano.
3. Divide mixture into six sections then roll each into a ball.

4. Press each ball down flat to form a patty.
5. Place patties on the pan and cook for approximately four minutes on each side or until cooked to your liking.
6. Place a slice of cheese on each cooked burger.
7. Place each burger on a large piece of lettuce.
8. Top with spread, one slice tomato, red onion and whatever else you like.
9. Wrap the lettuce up over the top.
10. Your dish is ready to be served.

4.5 Recipes for Juices, Sweet Dishes and Salads

Following are some juices, sweet dishes, and salad recipes rich in healthy nutrients that you can follow while being on the Optavia diet:

1) Vegetable Juice Recipe

Nutritional Value: 110 Calories

Preparation Time: 15 minutes

Cooking Time: 5 minutes

Serving: 4

Ingredients:

- Pealed ginger, one thumb size
- Lemon, one
- Celery stalks, four
- Cucumber, one
- Curly kale, one
- Granny smith apples, two

Instructions:
1. Wash all the ingredients.
2. Mix together in a food juicer.
3. Blend it for five minutes.
4. Pour the juice in glasses
5. Your juice is ready to be served.

2) Chia Bliss Smoothie Recipe

Nutritional Value: 132 Calories

Preparation Time: 10 minutes

Cooking Time: 5 minutes

Serving: 2

Ingredients:
- Chia seeds, a quarter cup
- Navitas cacao powder, two tbsp.
- Coconut milk, two cups
- Sweet nibs, one tbsp.
- Water, one cup
- Coconut palm sugar, two tbsp.
- Soft tofu, half cup

Instructions:
1. Wash the chia seeds.
2. Mix together in a food juicer.
3. Blend it for five minutes.
4. Pour the juice in glasses
5. Your smoothie is ready to be served.

3) Velvety Hot Chocolate Recipe

Nutritional Value: 147 Calories

Preparation Time: 10 minutes

Cooking Time: 5 minutes

Serving: 2

Ingredients:
- Protein powder, two tbsp.
- Unsweetened almond milk, two cups
- Vanilla extract, half tsp.
- Stevia extract powder, one tbsp.
- Galactomannan, half tsp.
- Butter, half tbsp.
- Cocoa powder, three tbsp.
- Water, two cups

Instructions:
1. Heat the liquid to the desired temperature.
2. Blend all ingredients together.
3. Be careful when blending hot liquids as they may expand and create a pressure build up.
4. Your dish is ready to be served.

4) Yoghurt Berry Blast Smoothie Recipe

Nutritional Value: 143 Calories

Preparation Time: 5 minutes

Cooking Time: 5 minutes

Serving: 2

Ingredients:

- Protein powder, one tbsp.
- Fresh blueberries, half cup
- Greek vanilla yoghurt, five ounces
- Milk, two cups
- Banana, one
- Strawberries, six

Instructions:

1. Using an immersion blender or blender, mix together the yogurt, banana and berries and slowly add in enough milk until slushy.
2. Just make sure the yogurt is just thawed and slushy.
3. Pour it into cups.
4. Your dish is ready to be served.

5) Peanut Butter Brownie Whoopi Pies Recipe

Nutritional Value: 210 Calories

Preparation Time: 20 minutes

Cooking Time: 10 minutes

Serving: 6

Ingredients:

- Eggs, two
- Milk, a quarter cup
- Vanilla flavor frosting, one cup
- Pure vegetable oil, half cup
- Brownie mix, one pack
- Peanut butter, one and a half cup

Instructions:

1. Preheat the oven to 350 degrees.
2. Line the cookie sheets with parchment paper.
3. Combine the brownie mix, oil and eggs in medium bowl.
4. Beat 30 to 40 strokes.
5. Drop by tablespoonful onto prepared cookie sheet about two inches apart.
6. Bake for ten minutes or until edges are set.
7. Let it cool down for two minutes on cookie sheet.
8. Remove to wire rack to cool completely.
9. Beat the frosting and peanut butter in medium bowl with electric mixer on medium speed until light and fluffy.
10. Add milk, beating until smooth.

11. Place half of pies flat side up.

12. Spoon two tablespoons filling in center of each pie.

13. Top with remaining pies, rounded side up.

14. Press gently to spread filling.

15. Your dish is ready to be served.

6) Mini Peanut Butter Cups Recipe

Nutritional Value: 110 Calories

Preparation Time: 10 minutes

Cooking Time: 30 minutes

Serving: 2

Ingredients:
- Maple syrup, two tbsp.
- Honey, two tbsp.
- Peanut butter, half cup
- Flaky sea salt, as required
- Chocolate, six ounces

Instructions:
1. In a small bowl, combine the peanut butter and maple syrup, and stir until well blended.
2. Fill a mini cupcake pan with liners or arrange mini cupcake liners on plate.
3. Melt the chocolate.
4. Fill the bottom of each cup with one teaspoon of the melted chocolate.

5. Add a small dollop of the peanut butter mixture in the center, and then top it with another teaspoon of the chocolate.
6. Freeze the candies for five minutes.
7. Sprinkle sea salt lightly over the tops, and then freeze until firm for twenty-five minutes more.
8. Store at room temperature for up to one week, or in the refrigerator for up to two months.
9. Your dish is ready to be served.

7) Mint Chocolate Cheesecake Muffins Recipe

Nutritional Value: 230 Calories

Preparation Time: 25 minutes

Cooking Time: 35 minutes

Serving: 12

Ingredients:

- Egg yolk, one
- All-purpose flour, one and a half cup
- Cream cheese, four ounces
- Cocoa powder, a quarter cup
- Cold water, one cup
- Granulated sugar, one cup
- Salt, half tsp.
- Baking soda, one tsp.
- Chopped chocolate mints, one cup
- White vinegar, one tbsp.
- Vanilla extract, one tsp.
- Oil, a quarter cup

Instructions:
1. Preheat the oven to 350 degrees.
2. Line a 12-count muffin tin with cupcake liners.
3. In a large bowl, whisk together the flour, baking soda, salt, cocoa powder and sugar.
4. Make three holes in the dry ingredients.
5. Measure the vanilla into the small holes, the vinegar into the medium, and the oil into the large.
6. Pour the cold water over top and whisk until the batter is smooth.
7. Add the softened cream cheese and egg yolk to a small bowl and whip using a handheld electric mixer on medium speed until smooth and creamy.
8. Fold in the chocolate mint pieces.
9. Fill each cupcake liner half full with the chocolate batter, then drop one to two teaspoons of cheesecake filling in the middle of each; finally cover with about one tablespoon of the remaining chocolate batter.
10. They should be filled all the way to the top with batter and cheesecake filling.
11. Bake the cupcakes in the preheated oven for thirty minute or until a toothpick inserted into the cake part around the edges of the cupcake comes out clean.
12. Let cool for ten minutes and then remove from the muffin tin to finish cooling on a wire rack.
13. Refrigerate until ready to serve.
14. These taste great when served with whipped cream on top.

15. Your dish is ready to be served.

8) Thin Mint Cookies Recipe

Nutritional Value: 180 Calories

Preparation Time: 10 minutes

Cooking Time: 10 minutes

Serving: 10

Ingredients:

- Pepper mint extract, half tsp.
- Sugar, three tbsp.
- Maple syrup, one tbsp.
- Vanilla extract, one tbsp.
- Cocoa powder, three tbsp.
- White flour, half cup
- Milk, one and a half tbsp.
- Vegetable oil, two tbsp.
- Salt, a pinch
- Baking soda, one tsp.
- Almond milk, one tbsp.

Instructions:

1. For the coating, you can either melt half cup chocolate chips or sugar free chocolate chips with peppermint extract and oil.
2. In a large bowl, combine the flour, cocoa, sugar, baking soda, and salt, and stir very well.

3. Whisk together all remaining cookie ingredients, pour wet into dry, and stir to form dough.
4. Refrigerate dough at least one hour.
5. Preheat oven to 300 degrees.
6. Lightly grease a baking sheet.
7. While the dough is still in the bag, roll it out with a rolling pin until it fills the bag.
8. Entirely cut away one side of the bag so that the dough is exposed.
9. Using a round cookie cutter or a lid cut out circles, and transfer to the baking sheet.
10. Bake for ten minutes.
11. They will look underdone, but they continue to cook as they cool.
12. Remove from the oven and allow to cool down for at least ten minutes before removing.
13. Dip cookies in chocolate coating.
14. Your cookies are ready to be served.

9) Mini Cranberry Orange Spiced Cheesecake Recipe

Nutritional Value: 218 Calories

Preparation Time: 30 minutes

Cooking Time: 15 minutes

Serving: 6

Ingredients:

- Toasted pecans, a quarter cup
- Granulated sugar, half cup

- Orange zest, one tbsp.
- Cream cheese, eight ounces
- Cookie crumbs, one cup
- Egg, one
- Vanilla extract, one tsp.
- Sour cream, one tbsp.
- Unsalted butter, four tbsp.
- Orange juice, two tbsp.
- Salt, a pinch
- Whipped cream, as required

Instructions:
1. Place the heavy whipping cream, sugar, and vanilla in the bowl of a stand mixer fitted with the whisk attachment and beat on medium high speed until soft peaks begin to form.
2. Remove the whisk attachment and whisk just a bit more by hand until you have reached the desired consistency.
3. Beat the cream cheese in a medium bowl until smooth for one minute.
4. Add the sugar, egg, sour cream or yogurt, orange juice, zest, and vanilla, and beat until smooth and well combined.
5. Fill each cavity with the filling as evenly as possible, and bake on the middle rack of the oven for twenty minutes or until set but slightly wobbly in the center.
6. Begin checking for doneness after ten minutes, as oven temperatures vary considerably.

7. Cool for twenty minutes on a wire rack, then using your finger, push up through the hole in the bottom of each cheesecake and remove each one.
8. Use a knife to loosen the sides if necessary.
9. Place the cheesecakes on a serving tray.
10. Pipe the whipped cream decoratively over the cheesecakes and top with the desired amount of orange sugared cranberries.
11. Garnish with more orange zest and serve with more orange sugared cranberries.
12. Your cheesecake is ready to be served.

10) Chocolate Pudding Recipe

Nutritional Value: 270 Calories

Preparation Time: 10 minutes

Cooking Time: 20 minutes

Serving: 4

Ingredients:
- Milk, three cups
- Vanilla extract, one tsp.
- White sugar, half cup
- Butter, two tbsp.
- Cornstarch, a quarter cup
- Cocoa powder, three tbsp.
- Salt, a pinch

Instructions:
1. In a pan, stir together sugar, cocoa, cornstarch and salt.
2. Place over medium heat, and stir in milk.

3. Bring to a boil, and cook, stirring constantly, until mixture thickens enough to coat the back of a metal spoon.
4. Remove from heat, and stir in butter and vanilla.
5. Let it cool in a refrigerator.
6. Your dish is ready to be served.

11) Chocolate Coconut Cream Pie Recipe

Nutritional Value: 310 Calories

Preparation Time: 50 minutes

Cooking Time: 60 minutes

Serving: 6

Ingredients:

- Sugar, six tbsp.
- Heavy cream, one cup
- Powdered sugar, three tbsp.
- Whole milk, two cups
- Bittersweet chocolate, seven ounces
- Corn starch, three tbsp.
- Piecrust, one package
- Egg yolks, four
- Vanilla extract, one tsp.
- Shredded coconut, one cup
- Chocolate shavings, half cup
- Salt, a pinch
- Butter, two and a half tbsp.

Instructions:

1. In a pan or microwave bring milk to a boil.
2. Meanwhile, in a large saucepan whisk the yolks with the sugar, cornstarch and salt until well blended and thick.
3. Whisking constantly, in a slow stream over medium heat, add the milk to the sugar mixture and bring to a boil.
4. Boil for two minutes and remove from heat.
5. Whisk in melted chocolate and let stand for five minutes.
6. Stir in butter until incorporated and smooth.
7. Press a piece of plastic wrap over the surface and refrigerate until chilled.
8. In a pan, over medium low heat, stir together heavy cream, shredded coconut and vanilla and bring to a boil.
9. Continue to cook the mixture until reduced by half and slightly thickened for five minutes.
10. When ready to assemble, place coconut cream mixture into the bottom of your cooled pie crust and spread evenly.
11. Quickly whisk the chocolate to loosen and pour over the coconut mixture, in an even layer.
12. If not serving immediately, place a piece of plastic wrap against the filling and refrigerate up to one hour.
13. Beat the heavy cream on high.
14. Turn down to low and add in powdered sugar, and vanilla.
15. Beat until stiff peaks.

16. Spread over the pie.
17. Top with toasted coconut, chocolate shavings.
18. Your pie is ready to be served.

12) Chocolate Peanut Butter Donuts Recipe

Nutritional Value: 182 Calories

Preparation Time: 20 minutes

Cooking Time: 10 minutes

Serving: 10

Ingredients:

- Baking soda, half tsp.
- Heavy cream, four tbsp.
- All-purpose flour, one cup
- Salt, a pinch
- Brown sugar, half cup
- Baking powder, one tsp.
- Unsalted butter, two tbsp.
- Buttermilk, one cup
- Eggs, two
- Peanut butter, three tbsp.
- Powdered sugar, one cup

Instructions:

1. Preheat oven to 350 degrees.
2. Lightly grease two donut pans with cooking spray.
3. In a large bowl, combine the flour, cocoa powder, brown sugar, baking powder, baking soda, and salt.

4. In a separate bowl, combine the eggs, buttermilk, and butter.
5. Whisk until well combined.
6. Add to flour mixture and mix just until moistened. Be careful not to over mix.
7. Pour mixture into a large zip-top bag and cut the corner off.
8. Pipe the mixture into the prepared pans, filling each donut mold.
9. Bake for ten minutes or until the donuts spring back when touched.
10. Allow the donuts to cool in the pans on a wire rack for ten minutes.
11. Place the butter and peanut butter in a small microwave-safe bowl.
12. Microwave for thirty seconds.
13. Stir vigorously to combine.
14. Stir the sugar into the peanut butter mixture.
15. Gradually stir in the cream one tablespoon at a time, stirring well after each addition, until the frosting is smooth.
16. The frosting will be thick.
17. Dip the tops of each donut into the frosting.
18. Use the back of a spoon to smooth the frosting if needed.
19. Your dish is ready to be served.

13) Chicken Cobb Salad Recipe

Nutritional Value: 131 Calories
Preparation Time: 10 minutes
Cooking Time: 10 minutes
Serving: 4

Ingredients:
- Cucumber, peeled and cubed, half cup
- Cherry tomatoes, cut in half
- Garbanzo beans, rinsed, one cup
- Cooked quinoa, a quarter cup
- Slivered almonds, three tbsp.
- Sunflower seeds to sprinkle on top
- Cracked pepper
- Romaine Lettuce, two
- Asparagus spears, cut, four grilled
- Green beans, cut, half cup
- Cubed roasted golden beets, half cup
- Avocado, cubed, half
- Grilled chicken cubes, one cup

Instructions:
1. Place the cut Romaine lettuce on plate.
2. Place all the cut vegetables in sections on the salad greens.

3. Mix the quinoa with the slivered almonds and place quinoa in the middle of the salad.
4. Add the chicken pieces above them.
5. Drizzle your preferred dressing on top and serve.

14) Shrimp Campechana Salad Recipe

Nutritional Value: 120 Calories

Preparation Time: 10 minutes

Cooking Time: 5 minutes

Serving: 2

Ingredients:
- Large shrimps, one pound
- Lime juice, a quarter cup
- Avocado, two
- Salt, as required
- Pepper, as required
- White onion, one
- Roma tomatoes, two
- Cilantro, a quarter cup
- Tomato sauce, half cup
- Tabasco pepper sauce, three tbsp.
- Jalapeno pepper, one

Instructions:
1. Bring three cups of water to a boil in 4-quart saucepan.
2. Then, add a teaspoon salt; cook shrimps in boiling water.

3. Remove from heat; drain, cool, then cut shrimps in half.
4. Combine tomato sauce, tomato, onion, jalapeño, cilantro, lime juice and Tabasco in a large glass bowl.
5. Add the cooked shrimps, and refrigerate at least for one hour.
6. Chop avocados coarsely.
7. Stir into shrimp mixture.
8. Your salad is ready to be served.

15) Chicken Caesar Salad Recipe

Nutritional Value: 130 Calories

Preparation Time: 10 minutes

Cooking Time: 10 minutes

Serving: 3

Ingredients:
- Garlic pepper, one tsp.
- Garlic minced and mashed, one clove
- Romaine lettuce, chopped
- Fresh shredded Asiago cheese
- Toasted croutons.
- Hellman's mayonnaise, half cup
- Finely grated parmesan cheese, half cup
- Buttermilk, a quarter cup
- Sweet and sour dressing, half cup
- Dry Ranch dressing mix, two tsp.

Instructions:
1. Combine the ingredients for the dressing.
2. Add dressing to the lettuce, to taste.
3. Mix well and refrigerate.
4. Serve topped with shredded Asiago cheese and toasted croutons.

16) Caprese Salad Recipe

Nutritional Value: 149 Calories

Preparation Time: 10 minutes

Cooking Time: 5 minutes

Serving: 2

Ingredients:
- Extra virgin olive oil, two tbsp.
- Grape tomatoes, half cup
- Sea salt, as required
- Fresh basil leaves, half cup
- Balsamic vinegar, one tbsp.
- Mozzarella cheese, four ounces

Instructions:
1. In a medium bowl, toss together the cut-up tomatoes, mozzarella, and basil leaves.
2. Add olive oil to bowl, and lightly toss together.
3. Drizzle the balsamic vinegar over the top of salad.
4. Sprinkle salt as desired.

17) Mediterranean Chicken Salad Recipe

Nutritional Value: 160 Calories

Preparation Time: 10 minutes

Cooking Time: 20 minutes

Serving: 4

Ingredients:
- Sundried tomatoes, a half cup
- Garlic, one
- Balsamic vinegar, two tbsp.
- Cooked chicken, two cups
- Chopped basil, two tbsp.
- Kalamata olives, half cup
- Salt, to taste
- Pepper, to taste
- Pine nuts, two tbsp.
- Mayonnaise, a quarter cup
- Butter lettuce, half cup
- Red bell pepper, one
- Red onion, two tbsp.
- Artichoke hearts, half cup

Instructions:

1. Separate each clove of garlic from the bulb and place them on a baking tray.
2. If making homemade roasted bell peppers, deseed the pepper, cut it into quarters and place on the baking tray.
3. Drizzle the garlic and pepper slices with olive oil and bake in the oven for twenty minutes.
4. While the garlic and peppers are cooking, chop the rest of the ingredients and add them to a bowl along with the chopped chicken.
5. Once the garlic is soft and caramelized, squeeze the garlic out of each clove and into a blender.
6. Add in the mayonnaise, balsamic vinegar, salt and pepper and blend until completely smooth.
7. Leave the roasted bell peppers to rest for a few minutes before peeling off the outer skins and chopping the peppers into small pieces.
8. Add them to the bowl with the other ingredients
9. Pour the dressing over the mixture and toss to ensure everything is well coated.
10. Spoon the chicken salad into lettuce cups and garnish with pine nuts and chopped basil before serving.
11. Your dish is ready to be served.

18) Lean and Green Tuna Salad Recipe

Nutritional Value: 117 Calories

Preparation Time: 5 minutes

Cooking Time: 5 minutes

Serving: 2

Ingredients:
- Hard boiled eggs, two
- Chopped onions, a quarter cup
- Lemon juice, as required
- Tuna, two cups
- Red bell pepper, half cup
- Hummus, a quarter cup
- Curry powder, one tsp.
- Cooked quinoa, half cup
- Cayenne pepper, one tsp.
- Salsa, three tbsp.
- Avocado, half cup

Instructions:
1. Combine the tuna, avocado and hummus in a bowl.
2. Add remaining ingredients and stir to combine.
3. Taste and adjust seasonings.
4. Your salad is ready to be served.

19) Avocado Chicken Salad Recipe

Nutritional Value: 260 Calories

Preparation Time: 10 minutes

Cooking Time: 5 minutes

Serving: 2

Ingredients:

- Avocados, one
- Arugula, a handful
- Lemon juice, half tsp.
- Red wine vinegar, half tsp.
- Lettuce leaf, half cup
- Extra virgin olive oil, two tbsp.
- Red onion, one
- Boiled chicken breasts, one cup
- Dijon mustard, half tsp.
- Oregano, two tbsp.
- Black pepper, as required
- Cherry tomatoes, half cup

Instructions:

1. Prepare the salad dressing my mixing together red wine vinegar, extra virgin olive oil, oregano, Dijon mustard, black pepper and lemon juice.
2. Peel the avocado and cut fine slices of it in a bowl.

3. Next, wash the cherry tomatoes and cut them into halves.
4. Peel and finely chop the red onion in a small bowl.
5. Then, finally cut the boiled chicken in julienne form.
6. Also, wash the arugula and lettuce leaves, and pat them dry.
7. Keep these salad leaves aside until required.
8. Once the salad dressing is ready, take a large bowl and throw in the washed arugula and lettuce leaves.
9. Add the finely chopped red onion, chicken along with halved cherry tomatoes and arugula slices in the bowl.
10. Pour the prepared dressing over it and toss well all the ingredients.
11. Your dish is ready to be served.

20) Tomato, Cucumber, and Cottage Cheese Salad Recipe

Nutritional Value: 107 Calories

Preparation Time: 10 minutes

Cooking Time: 30 minutes

Serving: 2

Ingredients:
- Cucumber, one cup
- Ground pepper, as required
- Tomatoes, two cups
- Cottage cheese, sixteen ounces

Instructions:

1. Wash and cut the tomatoes.
2. Wash the cucumbers and seed if desired.
3. Slice the cucumbers into small pieces.
4. Cut the cucumber into chunks.
5. Using a medium size bowl, preferably clear, layer the tomatoes, cucumber and cottage cheese.
6. Place in fridge until ready to serve.
7. Your salad is ready to be served.

21) Cranberry Honey Nut Granola Bar Recipe

Nutritional Value: 283 Calories

Preparation Time: 10 minutes

Cooking Time: 31 minutes

Serving: 6

Ingredients:

- Honey, half cup
- Vanilla extract, one tsp.
- Oats, two cups
- Ground flax seeds, half cup
- Pecan, half cup
- Chocolate chips, one cup
- Dried cranberries, one cup
- Brown sugar, one cup
- Vegetable oil, two tbsp.
- Wheat germ, a quarter cup
- Cinnamon, half tsp.

- Salt, to taste

Instructions:
1. Preheat the oven to 350 degrees.
2. Stir brown sugar, honey, vegetable oil, and salt together in a large microwave-safe bowl.
3. Mix oats, cranberries, pecans, ground flax seed, chocolate chips, and wheat germ together in a bowl.
4. Stir mixture and heat in microwave again until smooth.
5. Stir vanilla extract and cinnamon into brown sugar mixture.
6. Stir brown sugar mixture into oats mixture until evenly mixed and chocolate is melted; pour into the prepared baking dish.
7. Bake in the preheated oven until edges are golden brown for thirty minutes.
8. Lift bars out of pan by pulling by the parchment paper.
9. Cool for five minutes before cutting into bars.
10. Your bars are ready to be served.

22) Chocolate Mint Cookie Crisp Bar Recipe

Nutritional Value: 227 Calories

Preparation Time: 10 minutes

Cooking Time: 30 minutes

Serving: 6

Ingredients:
- Almond butter, a quarter cup
- Dark cocoa powder, one tbsp.
- Rice crisp cereal, two cups
- Mint extract, a quarter tsp.
- Raw amber agave, half cup
- Semi-sweet chocolate chips, a quarter cup
- Vanilla extract, one tsp.
- Salt, a pinch

Instructions:
1. In a large bowl, combine the rice cereal and chocolate chips.
2. In a small pot, add the almond butter, agave, cocoa powder and salt and whisk very well until smooth.
3. Turn the heat to medium and bring to a simmer.
4. Once the edges begin to simmer, whisk constantly for just about a minute until it begins to thicken.
5. Remove from heat and stir in the vanilla and mint extracts.

6. Now, pour the heated mixture over the dry ingredients and stir quickly because it will start to harden.
7. This will melt the chocolate chips, which additionally will help to harden the bars.
8. Press mixture down flat and hard into the pan with the back of a spoon, spread out evenly.
9. Chill in the fridge at least thirty minutes and slice with a sharp knife into bars.
10. Keep them stored in the fridge to retain their shape.
11. Your dish is ready to be served.

23) Zesty Lemon Crisp Bar Recipe

Nutritional Value: 227 Calories

Preparation Time: 10 minutes

Cooking Time: 30 minutes

Serving: 6

Ingredients:
- Almond butter, a quarter cup
- Rice crisp cereal, two cups
- Raw amber agave, half cup
- Lemon zest, a quarter cup
- Vanilla extract, one tsp.
- Salt, a pinch

Instructions:

1. In a large bowl, combine the rice cereal lemon zest.
2. In a small pot, add the almond butter, agave and salt and whisk very well until smooth.
3. Turn the heat to medium and bring to a simmer.
4. Once the edges begin to simmer, whisk constantly for just about a minute until it begins to thicken some.
5. Remove from heat and stir in the vanilla extract.
6. Now, pour the heated mixture over the dry ingredients and stir quickly because it will start to harden.
7. Press mixture down flat and hard into the pan with the back of a spoon, spread out evenly.
8. Chill in the fridge at least thirty minutes and slice with a sharp knife into bars.
9. Keep them stored in the fridge to retain their shape.
10. Your dish is ready to be served.

24) Frosted Cookie Dough Bar Recipe

Nutritional Value: 221 Calories

Preparation Time: 20 minutes

Cooking Time: 25 minutes

Serving: 6

Ingredients:

- Vanilla extract, half tsp.
- All-purpose flour, two cups
- Heavy cream, four tbsp.
- Butter, three quarter cups
- Baking powder, one tsp.

- Eggs, two
- Powdered sugar, one cup
- Granulated sugar, one cup
- Salt, a pinch

Instructions:

1. Using an electric mixer on medium speed, beat the sugar and flour until thoroughly combined.
2. Add three tablespoons cream and the vanilla.
3. Continue beating, adding more cream a small amount at a time, until the frosting is the desired consistency.
4. Preheat the oven to 350 degrees.
5. Whisk together the flour, baking powder, and salt.
6. Using an electric mixer on medium speed, beat the butter and sugar until light and fluffy. Add the eggs, one at a time, mixing well after each addition.
7. Mix in the vanilla.
8. Reduce mixer speed to low.
9. Gradually add the flour mixture, mixing just until combined.
10. Spread the batter in the prepared pan.
11. Bake for twenty minutes.
12. Spread the frosting on the cooled bars.
13. Your dish is ready to be served.

25) Chocolate Fudge Crisp Bar Recipe

Nutritional Value: 181 Calories

Preparation Time: 10 minutes

Cooking Time: 15 minutes

Serving: 6

Ingredients:
- Cinnamon, a pinch
- Butter, six tbsp.
- Cayenne pepper, a pinch
- Powdered sugar, one cup
- Corn syrup, a quarter cup
- Crisp rice cereal, three cups
- Vanilla extract, one tsp.
- Chocolate chips, one and a half cup

Instructions:
1. Lightly butter or line with waxed paper.
2. In a saucepan, combine the butter, corn syrup, chocolate chips, cinnamon and cayenne.
3. Cook over low heat, stirring constantly, until smooth.
4. Remove from heat.
5. Stir in the vanilla extract and powdered sugar, mixing until smooth.
6. Add the cereal and mix well.
7. Spread in prepared pan.

8. Refrigerate until well chilled and completely set.
9. Cut into bars.
10. Your dish is ready to be served.

26) Raisin Oat Cinnamon Crisp Bar Recipe

Nutritional Value: 231 Calories

Preparation Time: 15 minutes

Cooking Time: 30 minutes

Serving: 8

Ingredients:

- Baking soda, one tsp.
- Butter, one and a half cup
- Baking powder, one tsp.
- Light brown sugar, one cup
- All-purpose flour, two cups
- Salt, a pinch
- Granulated sugar, one cup
- Dark brown sugar, half cup
- Vanilla extract, one tsp.
- Nutmeg, a quarter tsp.
- Raisins, one cup
- Rolled oats, two cups
- Cinnamon, one tsp.
- Eggs, one

Instructions:

1. Heat the oven.
2. Mix the flour, salt, baking soda, and baking powder together into a large mixing bowl.
3. Mix in the eggs one at a time, then add the vanilla, cinnamon, and nutmeg.
4. Beat the butter, brown sugar, dark brown sugar, and granulated sugar in until fluffy.
5. Mix in the flour mixture and mix until combined.
6. Stir in the oats by hand, followed by the raisins.
7. Spread dough evenly into the pan.
8. Spread the dough into the prepared pan and smooth the top.
9. Bake for thirty minutes.
10. Remove from the oven and let cool ten minutes before cutting.
11. Your dish is ready to be served.

27) Raisin Oat Cinnamon Crisp Bar Recipe

Nutritional Value: 35 Calories

Preparation Time: 5 minutes

Cooking Time: 60 minutes

Serving: 8

Ingredients:

- Greek yoghurt, three cups
- Honey, two tbsp.
- Fresh strawberries, three

Instructions:

1. Place the strawberries in the food processor and process until finely chopped.
2. Carefully remove the blade.
3. Add the yogurt and honey.
4. Use the small scoop to transfer the mixture into holes of the snack bar maker
5. Cover and chill in the freezer for one hour or overnight.
6. Remove the bars from the tray and then return them to the freezer to store.
7. Your dish is ready to be served.

28) Chocolate Caramel Delight Crisp Bar Recipe

Nutritional Value: 113 Calories

Preparation Time: 30 minutes

Cooking Time: 10 minutes

Serving: 8

Ingredients:

- Whipping cream, three tbsp.
- Pecans, one cup
- Vanilla caramels, sixteen
- Butter, half cup
- Milk, two tbsp.
- Sugar, half cup
- Vanilla extract, one tsp.
- Egg, one

- Unsweetened cocoa powder, half cup
- Unsweetened Chocolate pieces, half cup
- Shortening, one tsp.

Instructions:
1. In a large mixing bowl, beat the butter.
2. Beat in egg yolk, milk and vanilla.
3. In another bowl, stir together the flour, cocoa powder and salt.
4. Add the flour mixture to butter mixture and beat till well combined.
5. In a small saucepan, heat and stir caramels and whipping cream over low heat till mixture is smooth.
6. Slightly beat reserved white.
7. Roll the balls in egg white, then in nuts to coat.
8. Place an inch apart on a lightly greased cookie sheet.
9. Using your thumb, make an indentation in the center of each cookie.
10. Bake on 350 degrees.
11. Spoon some melted caramel mixture into indentation of each cookie.
12. Transfer cookies to wire rack to cool.
13. In another saucepan, heat and stir chocolate pieces and shortening over low heat till chocolate is melted and mixture is smooth.
14. Transfer the chocolate mixture to a self-sealing plastic bag.
15. Close bag and cut a small hole in one corner of it.

16. Drizzle cookies with chocolate mixture.
17. Your dish is ready to be served.

Conclusion

Weight decrease has been in design for an extensively lengthy timespan now. It appears to be that everybody is eager to get thinner. You can follow numerous eating regimens that are accessible on the web. All things considered, every one of them will empty out your energy saves and leave you undesirable, draining your nutrients and mineral stores.

This book invites you to a universe of solid and scrumptious eating. In the first section, we talked about the science behind good dieting, and we found the universe of sustenance and dietetics. The set of experiences behind the commencement of the study of food and diet was additionally contemplated. This book gave a top to bottom investigate the science and idea driving Optavia diet.

Optavia diet follows the principle of eating a combination of some very low caloric meals and a few high caloric meals making sure to not exceed 1000 to 1200 calories per day. In this way, a person is not deprived of the essential nutrients and energy that he needs to carry out his daily routine.

Optavia diet can be trailed by everybody aside from some vulnerable people, as it might have numerous unfavorable impacts on their bodies. Optavia diet includes two stages for the decrease of weight and how this work does logically is referenced in section two. This book will help you in decreasing load by giving you numerous wondrous thoughts and plans that you can make effectively at your home with no issue. The recipes include breakfast, snacks, meals just as sweet dishes and squeezes are referenced to fulfill your desires just as give you a decent guide for lessening weight. You can without much of a stretch expands your cooking by picking your favored dinner and while keeping in mind the calorie level for that particular dish.

Eventually, we talked about numerous systems and strategies that can be picked all together to diminish the weight as well as keep up that decreased weight. Keeping yourself inspired during abstains from food is the main activity; without inspiration, you might be going no place. Keeping a sound body should be the first concern of each person, and this book can give you a stunning rule for accomplishing all your weight and wellbeing related objectives with tips and deceives concerning weight support and receiving a solid, dynamic and positive way of life.

CPSIA information can be obtained
at www.ICGtesting.com
Printed in the USA
BVHW072017270421
605952BV00012B/1031